Cook and Ladder

A Collection of Recipes from your Neighborhood Firehouse Kitchen

Michael B. Riley, Sr.

Driver/Engineer/Paramedic (retired)

Rockford, IL. Fire Department

Thank you, first off, to my wife Heather. For putting up with me all these years, for helping me eat everything I cooked as I nailed down the amounts for ingredients so every recipe wasn't filled with a bunch of "to taste" with no guidelines for a starting point, for being the strength I needed when I didn't think I had it, THANK YOU!

To those who are too numerous to mention that I learned to cook from, to those that I got recipes from through the years, to everyone I had the pleasure to cook for at the various clubhouses, THANK YOU!

Last and certainly not least, to Uncle Mark and my daughter Shani for acting as editors to help me be grammatically correct while still coming across in a written voice that sounds like me; and Scotty for creating a cover that was both exactly what I wanted yet better in every way, THANK YOU!

Table of Contents

II

IV

VI

Introduction

In 1736, Ben Franklin and others formed what is recognized as the first volunteer fire company in the United States. Volunteer fire halls became, and continue to be, neighborhood gathering places. The first kitchens in fire halls were used to cook for fundraisers to supplement or even provide the entire funding for these organizations. The firehouse kitchen took on a new importance in 1853 when Cincinnati formed the first fully paid full time Fire Department in the United States.

Firefighting has never been a "9 to 5" type of job, but in those early days it was not unusual for firefighters to work 23 hours a day, 6 days a week. They were allowed to go home for an hour for dinner, but if a fire call came in they were obliged to respond. One meal a day does not prepare someone for the rigors of fighting a fire, so the kitchen took on a different importance. Not only is the kitchen where the food is prepared, but it is also where the food is consumed by the entire shift, eating together as a family. This helps to fuel the teamwork necessary to coordinate activities on a fire scene, teamwork that allows firefighters to complete their primary missions, saving lives and property.

That spirit continues today, where in fire stations across the United States right now someone is busy cooking a meal for the benefit of their crew. Some stations shop for their groceries on duty, taking their apparatus to the store (while remaining in radio contact, ready to respond to emergencies) while at others the cook for the day stops on the way into work and brings the groceries with them. Regardless of which method, the firefighters partaking in the meals contribute towards the cost of the meals. The department does not pay for the meals, just as most employers do not pay for their employees' meals while they are at work.

For a number of years, I was the designated cook for the various stations I was assigned to. Cooking isn't the only thing the cook has to do for the day. The day's cook still has to perform all the normal duties for their position in the department, whether it's the new guy having to clean the toilets (regardless of how much seniority I had, I always offered to clean the toilets for the cook, for obvious reasons), the Driver/Engineer checking over the apparatus (my position for the last nine years of my career), or the Officer, having to do all the paperwork and everything else involved with their position.

My first several years I was on the department I had the good fortune to work with some of the best cooks our department has seen. I was able to learn from them a style of cooking I was not familiar with, cooking from scratch with some short cuts along the way. Before becoming the designated cook, I would go to the store, find which proteins were on sale (with the protein being the most expensive part of the meal) and build a couple meals around that. Once I became the designated cook, I developed themes for each day for one of the meals. I then left the other meal open for whatever was on sale, or whatever I felt like cooking that day.

Sunday became Sugo Sunday (Sugo being the Italian for gravy, American Italian for tomato sauce), followed by Meatloaf Monday, Taco Tuesday, Wing Wednesday, Tot Waffle Thursday, Fish Friday (or Fajita Friday when I worked with someone that didn't like seafood), and Pizza Saturday. I have multiple recipes for each day's theme, making the decisions at the store easier first thing in the morning while keeping a variety for the guys (and gals) that I was feeding. The most important thing you have to account for is making sure you have the quantity of food to feed your entire crew of firefighters, then it must be at least edible if not good. All of my recipes make enough to feed six hungry firefighters. Two things make the food instantly better – one is if your meal is delayed due to multiple emergency runs, the other is reheating the leftovers after returning from a fire.

Follow me on Instagram (cookandladdercono1), and my Facebook page (Cook & Ladder Co. No. 1) where you can share pictures when you make my recipes, as well as post your firehouse recipes. 10% of net proceeds from the sale of this book will be donated to Fire Department Coffee Foundation https://www.firedeptcoffee.com/ to help support firefighters and other first responders who are injured on the job, mentally or physically, or who are facing other serious health challenges. I hope you enjoy my recipes as much as the guys (and gals) I have fed through the years told me they did!

Fire Vocabulary, Part 1

In the fire service just within the United States, not to mention internationally, there may be several terms for the same thing. For the first section instead of the normal term followed by definition I've flipped this around to make things easier to understand. This is by no means a definitive list since various regions, even departments within the same region, often have different terms for the same thing.

Accountability check on emergency scene – PAR (Personal Accountability Report), PAC (Personal Accountability Check), Roll call

Aerial Ladder apparatus – Ladder, Tower, Truck

Crew on emergency scene dedicated to firefighter rescue – RIT (Rapid Intervention Team), RIC (Rapid Intervention Crew), RIG (Rapid Intervention Group), the original purpose of Squad companies

Device that can be connected to in order to receive water – Hydrant, plug

Engine apparatus – Engine, Pumper, Triple

Fire hose – Line, pipe, hoseline, almost never called hose

Firefighter assigned to a ladder company – Truckie, ladderman, knuckle dragger. Most departments have more Engines than Ladders, so even though ladder work is critical, they tend to get made fun of by the Engine guys.

Firefighter assigned to drive apparatus – Driver, Engineer, Driver/Engineer, Chauffeur, FEO (Fire Equipment Operator), FAO (Fire Apparatus Operator)

Geographic area company is expected to be first to a scene – Still, first due district, first in area

Group of firefighters assigned to work on a certain day – Shift, platoon

Large tractor/trailer apparatus with separate steering wheel for trailer – Tractor Drawn Aerial, Tiller, Tiller Truck, Hook and Ladder

Large water nozzle attached to apparatus (usually on top) – Deck gun, Deluge nozzle

Large water nozzle not attached to apparatus – Monitor, Ground hugger, Multi-versal, Master stream

Personal protective equipment for fighting fires – Bunker gear, Turnout gear, Hitch

Preconnected hose load across the apparatus above shoulder level – Crosslay, transverse lay

Preconnected hose load across the apparatus at shoulder level – Speedlay, Mattydale (named after the town in New York credited with inventing it)

Pre-fire plan to determine how to fight a fire at a particular location – Preplan, duty inspection, still inspection

Roadway collision – MVA (Motor vehicle accident), MVC (Motor Vehicle Collision), 10-50, PI Accident (Personal Injury Accident), Accident with injuries

Scheduled day of work – shift, trick, workday

Smaller apparatus designed for fighting grass fires – Grass Wagon, Grass Truck, A-Wagon, Brush Truck

When more resources are required on a scene – Extra Alarm, Box Alarm, Second (and Third, Fourth, etc…) Alarm, 2-11 (or 3-11, 4-11, etc…), Mutual Aid

Working fire – A job, a go, a burner, 10-80

Sugo Sunday

Anybody that had to cook at the station had their own Sugo recipe because it allowed the cook to basically make one meal that extended to the second meal. This was a good thing for two reasons – the cook only had to be in the kitchen all morning instead of morning and afternoon, and the Sugo always tasted better after more time for the flavors to meld. Every workday at the station required starting out checking over all the equipment you are responsible for, cleaning assigned spaces around the station, as well as responding to emergency calls. Monday through Friday also included other duties, such as pre-fire planning inspections, training, and bigger station cleaning and maintenance duties. Saturday was not as busy as the rest of the week, but still usually included bigger scope training than during the week. It was always nice to be able to take the afternoon off on Sundays, free to enjoy watching football, hockey, or other sports, usually as a group.

Pasta with Sugo

I prefer my sugo on the thick and chunky side – if you like yours thinner, substitute tomato sauce for the tomato puree and the tomato paste. If the chunks of tomatoes turn you off, leave them out. Like all of my recipes, this feeds six hungry firefighters, but this one does it for two meals.

2 Tablespoons olive oil
2 sweet onions, rough chop
3 cloves garlic, run through garlic press
1 can tomato puree, 105 ounces
3 cans (18 ounces each) tomato paste
2 cans (28 ounces each) diced tomatoes
1 pound button mushrooms (optional)
12 hard boiled eggs (optional)
2 Tablespoons oregano (or to taste)
2 Tablespoons basil (or to taste)
Pasta of choice ($^1/_4$ pound per person – your mileage may vary, but mine works for hungry firefighters)

Pour olive oil into big pot over medium low flame on stove
When oil shimmers, add onions
When onions are just about soft, add garlic
Stir constantly so garlic doesn't burn
When onions are soft, add all tomatoes, bring to boil
Add mushrooms and hard boiled eggs if using, lower sugo to simmer and cover
If you have fire bricks, place pot on them over low flame
Add oregano and basil, stir every once in a while until it's time to eat.

To cook the pasta –
Put pasta in a pot, cover with salted water, bring to a boil
Stir, turn off the heat, and cover
After 10 minutes, check if the pasta is done to your liking
Drain, return to pot, mix in a couple ladlefuls of the sugo
Top pasta with sugo, meatballs, and sausage, and Mangia!

Meatballs

Pasta and sugo will taste great, but without some meat it won't keep you full very long. I always figured on four meatballs per person for both meals, with about 8 meatballs per pound of meat. The recipe below gives you the amounts for 6 hungry firefighters for two meals. If you're able to, become friendly with your neighborhood butcher. A couple of the butchers at the meat counter at my local specialty grocery store got used to seeing me on a regular basis and would grind meat to order for me. If they're able to grind the beef and pork together for you, then you have to fuss with it less, making better meatballs.

1 $\frac{1}{2}$ pounds ground chuck (80/20)
1 $\frac{1}{2}$ pounds ground pork
$\frac{3}{4}$ cup grated parmesan cheese
2 large eggs, beaten
1 ladleful of sugo

Preheat oven to 350F
Mix all the ingredients
Roll out the meatballs
Place on cookie sheet
Cook for 30 minutes

To make life easier, you can throw links of Italian sausage in the oven with the meatballs, then just add all of them to the Sugo as it simmers

Lasagna

Even though this really belongs on Wednesday, it doesn't fit in with the wing theme, so here it is with Sunday Sugo. Since the crew pays for the groceries, any place you can save a little money without sacrificing quantity or quality is a good thing. If you have leftover Sugo after Sunday, you can use it on Wednesday for lasagna. This recipe assumes you have leftover meatballs and/or sausage in your Sugo. If not, just brown a mix of ground beef and bulk Italian sausage.

2 (15 ounce) containers ricotta cheese
2 cups shredded mozzarella cheese, divided
$1/2$ cup grated parmesan cheese, divided
2 large eggs, beaten
Leftover sugo
12 "no boil" lasagna noodles

Preheat oven to 375F
Mix ricotta, half of the mozzarella, half of the parmesan, and the eggs; set aside
Separate the leftover Sugo in half, one half with meat and one without meat
Use potato masher to break meat into small pieces
Spread half of meatless Sugo on bottom of 9" x 13" casserole dish
Layer 4 uncooked noodles, then half of the cheese mix followed by half of the Sugo with meat
Repeat – 4 uncooked noodles, remaining half of cheese mix, then remaining half of Sugo with meat
Top with last four uncooked noodles and remaining meatless Sugo
Bake, covered, for one hour
Remove cover, sprinkle with remaining mozzarella and parmesan cheeses
Bake uncovered ten more minutes
Let rest ten minutes before slicing and serving

A Day at the Station

One of the questions I was asked most often once someone found out I was a Firefighter was, "What the hell do you guys do all day?" The shift structure my department used was 24 hours on, 48 hours off. The following is the routine for a 24 hour shift – there are various other schedules used but this is the one I'm familiar with.

No two days were ever the same, but there were things that we accomplished every day. Once everybody's gear was checked and on the rig, everyone from both shifts gathered at the kitchen table to pass on not only what happened around the station over the past two days, but to "chew the fat" about anything and everything going on in the world. The daily newspaper would be the guide, and coffee worked as a social lubricant. Many of the world's problems have been solved at the Firehouse kitchen table, if only those in charge would listen to us. When the previous shift would leave to go home, that day's shift would stay at the table and catch up on each other's lives, such as who took their old man fishing yesterday, or the dumbass kid that scratched the hell out of the car backing out of the garage.

Once that part of the day was over, it was time to do the daily chores. Most stations do not have a cleaning crew other than the firefighters that work there. Daily chores are divided by position and seniority, and include everything from the aforementioned cleaning the toilets to mopping floors to checking over the rigs and ensuring they are in a state of readiness to respond to any emergency that the crew may get called to.

After the daily chores were finished, we'd usually wash the rigs and go right into our weekly chore for the day. There are some things that need to be taken care of on a normal basis, but not daily, such as checking over all the tools on the rigs, mowing the lawn, cleaning the apparatus floor, etc… Each day of the week was dedicated to one of these tasks, with the whole crew pitching in. You may notice that most things we did involved the whole crew, which helped to increase our bond from merely teammates to family. There may be times your brother or sister isn't your favorite person in the world, but you'd go to Hell and back for them and you have no doubt they'd do the same for you.

The weekly chore led to one of the milestones of the workday – Dinner. The goal was to have Dinner ready by 11:15-11:30. This allowed time for everyone to eat, determine who had to do the dishes, actually do the dishes, and be done by noon. This was important because from noon to 1:00pm was break time, with some people studying, some watching the news, some taking a quick power nap, and others just taking the time to sit in a chair and take a load off.

Around 1:00pm was when the training started. We did about three hours of training every workday as a company, on subjects ranging from a new tool or piece of equipment to the most basic act of firefighting from Day 1 of initial training. The officer in charge of the company usually chose the drill for the day, and the ones I liked working with the most had all members of the company take turns leading the training. You never truly know a subject until you have to teach it to someone else, and sometimes the newer guys would end up updating us senior guys on something that changed since we had been trained in it.

After 4:00pm, the day was yours. Some guys would get a quick workout in before supper, some would go back to studying, basically as long as you showed up at the truck quickly and dressed for the occasion when the bell went off, you could do what you wanted.

The goal for supper was to eat by 5:15-5:30pm. After the Supper dishes were done, then aside from the occasional multicompany Night drill you were free to spend your time as you wished.

Amongst all the above, we went on calls both emergency and nonemergency, did preplans, gave tours of the station, and did whatever we needed to do to keep the station running. And no, not once during my almost 26 years did I see anyone sitting around playing checkers.

Meatloaf Monday

Meatloaf is one of the most basic, yet most fulfilling meals around. Who can't help but be brought back to childhood by a nice, hot slab of meatloaf? There are hundreds of meatloaf recipes out there, and I've found that the absolute best one is usually the one your Mom made. All of my meatloaf recipes start with the same base – $3/4$ pound of meat per person, evenly split between 80/20 ground chuck and ground pork. The guys at the meat counter came in handy again here, because the less you have to handle the meatloaf to get all the ingredients mixed together, the better. One egg, along with $1/2$ cup binder (I usually evenly split bread crumbs and grated parmesan cheese) per two pounds of meat does the trick. You might find your family eats less than a bunch of hungry firefighters, so adjust your amounts accordingly. If you want to make your meatloaf as low carb as possible, use only grated parmesan and eggs for your binder. If you're making small amounts, you can pack your meatloaf into a 9" x 5" bread pan, or if you're making large amounts, I stumbled on a little trick to help keep your meatloaf uniform in size so it cooks evenly. Lay down plastic wrap in a 9" x 13" casserole dish, pack the meatloaf into the dish, then turn upside down onto a parchment paper lined cookie sheet. Remove the 9" x 13" and the plastic wrap, and you have an even loaf. When you get right down to it, it's meatloaf – pretty much the only way to screw it up is under cook it or over cook it.

Most Basic Meatloaf

Sometimes you just don't have time to follow a complex recipe, so with a minimum of ingredients here is your most basic meatloaf recipe. You can jazz it up by adding thinly sliced celery, shredded carrots, mushrooms, olives, whatever you have laying around and feel like adding. Just keep in mind you don't want to end up with more "stuff" than meat – the more "stuff" you add, the less of each kind of "stuff" you should add. I got this recipe from a coworker, who got it from his Mom. His Mom would put hard boiled eggs in the meatloaf, so each slice usually had a surprise in it. Boy, were we surprised when his meatloaf was crunchy – he forgot to peel the shells off the eggs!

2 pounds ground chuck (80/20)
2 pounds ground pork
1 sweet onion, diced small
2 eggs, beaten
1 cup milk
1 cup seasoned bread crumbs
1 cup ketchup (or enough to cover loaf)

Preheat oven to 350F
Combine meat, onion, eggs, milk and bread crumbs
Form into loaf
Bake for 1 hour, pull from oven, cover with ketchup
Bake for 15 more minutes
When internal temperature is 155F, pull from oven
Let rest on countertop until internal temperature is 165F
Slice and enjoy!

Mushroom Bacon Swiss Meatloaf

On page 130, you'll find my "Rileybuger" recipe. This meatloaf recipe was my way of still being able to have "Rileyburgers" when it was too cold out to grill.

1 $\frac{1}{2}$ pounds chopped raw bacon
1 sweet onion, rough chop
10 button mushrooms, chopped
1 $\frac{1}{2}$ pounds ground chuck (80/20)
1 $\frac{1}{2}$ pounds ground pork
2 eggs, beaten
$\frac{3}{4}$ pound swiss cheese, cubed
1 cup crushed pretzel pieces
$\frac{1}{2}$ pound swiss cheese, sliced

Preheat oven to 350F
Place bacon in a skillet and cook over medium heat until browned
Remove with a slotted spoon to paper towels
Discard all but 1 tablespoon of bacon grease
Stir onions and mushrooms into bacon grease, cook until soft
Mix all ingredients except about 1/8 of the bacon and the sliced cheese
Form into loaf
Bake for 1 hour, pull from oven, cover with sliced cheese and remaining bacon
Bake for 10 more minutes
When internal temperature is 155F, pull from oven
Let rest on countertop until internal temperature is 165F
Slice and enjoy!

Bacon Cheeseburger Meatloaf

If you're looking for a more conventional meatloaf take on a cheeseburger, here's your recipe! Another option is replacing the ketchup and mustard with barbecue sauce.

1 $^1/_2$ pounds chopped raw bacon
$^2/_3$ cup ketchup
$^1/_4$ cup prepared yellow mustard
1 $^1/_2$ pounds ground chuck (80/20)
1 $^1/_2$ pounds ground pork
2 (8 ounces each) packages shredded cheddar cheese
2 eggs, beaten
$^1/_2$ cup seasoned bread crumbs
$^1/_2$ cup grated parmesan cheese
$^1/_2$ cup mayonnaise
2 Tablespoons worcestershire sauce
2 (3 ounces each) can french-fried onions

Preheat oven to 350F
Place bacon in a large skillet and cook over medium-high heat, stirring occasionally, until evenly browned, about 10 minutes
Drain the bacon on paper towels. When cool, crumble into a large bowl
Mix ketchup and mustard in a bowl
Thoroughly combine $^1/_4$ the ketchup/mustard mixture, beef and pork, cheddar cheese, eggs, bread crumbs, mayonnaise, and worcestershire sauce with crumbled bacon in bowl
Form into loaf
Bake for 1 hour, pull from oven
Cover with rest of ketchup mixture and french-fried onions
Bake for 10 more minutes
When internal temperature is 155F, pull from oven
Let rest on countertop until internal temperature is 165F
Slice and enjoy!

Best Ever Meatloaf

More often than not, if I'm making meatloaf, it's this recipe. Not to denigrate any of my other meatloaf recipes, but this is my wife's favorite, so it's the one I go to most. The tomato soup keeps it moist while adding flavor, and the onion soup mix contributes a unique twang. The ketchup mixture on top provides the proverbial icing on the cake.

2 pounds ground chuck (80/20)
2 pounds ground pork
1 (10.75 ounce) can condensed tomato soup
$\frac{1}{2}$ cup seasoned bread crumbs
$\frac{1}{2}$ cup grated parmesan cheese
2 eggs, beaten
2 envelopes dry onion soup mix
$\frac{1}{2}$ cup ketchup
$\frac{1}{4}$ cup yellow mustard
$\frac{1}{4}$ cup brown sugar

Preheat oven to 350F
Mix meat, soup, bread crumbs, parmesan, eggs, and soup mix
Form into loaf
Bake for 1 hour, pull from oven
Mix ketchup, mustard, and brown sugar
Cover with ketchup mixture
Bake for 10 more minutes
When internal temperature is 155F, pull from oven
Let rest on countertop until internal temperature is 165F
Slice and enjoy!

The Engine

A Fire Engine is the most common type of fire apparatus. If a small department only has one rig, it's going to be an Engine. The main jobs an Engine must perform are to get the crew to the scene, provide water and hose to fight the fire, and carry tools to accomplish the other tasks encountered. Many departments also use their Engines as first response EMS vehicles. Every department designs their Engine(s) for the unique challenges they face.

Engines have changed greatly over the past century plus, going from hand drawn, hand pumped carts to the latest "Clean Cab" diesel powered rigs. The first advance was steam powered pumps pulled by a team of horses. Horses were eventually replaced by either the vehicle also being powered by steam or by gasoline. It was often a day of mixed emotions when the horses were fully replaced. There was excitement for the advancement of technology, yet sadness for the replacing of the tried and true. Eventually diesel fuel was determined to be a safer, more reliable way to power fire apparatus. Safety for the crew that rode on the apparatus was less of a concern. Rigs did not have roofs, only had seating for the Engineer and the Officer with everyone else having to ride on the back step of the rig, holding on for dear life. Most didn't even have seatbelts for the lucky ones that had seats. Eventually roofs started to appear, then seats for the whole crew, leading to today's fully enclosed rigs.

Originally, Engines were dependent on a water supply before being able to pump water. Nowadays, Engines carry 500+ gallons of water to give those fighting the fire a head start before gaining a water supply. Some departments have the first Engine to a working fire catch their own hydrant on their way to the fire, while some leave that responsibility to the second arriving Engine. Engines carry various sizes of hose, ranging from booster lines that are ¾" to 1" diameter, through attack lines ranging from 1 ½" to 3", up to supply lines as big as 5". Depending on the area served, some Engines also carry hard suction hose, which allows them to draw water from a static supply such as a lake, dry hydrant, or portable tank.

There is certain equipment Engines are required to carry, but that is just a minimum and is usually regarded as a starting point. The minimum equipment includes extinguishers, basic hand tools, forcible entry tools, ladders, and master stream devices. The hazards that the crew of the Engine may face determine the types and amounts of the extra equipment carried. Some Engines are also responsible for extrication, requiring hydraulic, electric, and pneumatic rescue tools; some are near bodies of water and carry extra water rescue equipment. Even in departments that try to have everything standardized there are small differences of what is carried and where it is carried, so it is fair to say Fire Engines are like snowflakes – no two are the same.

EMS is a huge part of the modern fire service. Even the cities that only sent a fire company if the ambulance got to a scene and found they needed help are now sending the nearest piece of fire equipment to arrive and start care before ambulance arrival. It is becoming more and more rare to find a "zero" – someone with no certification or responsibility other than being a firefighter. The "zero" by no means denigrates the holder of the title, it just means they have zero after their firefighter title. Not Firefighter/EMT, or Firefighter/Paramedic, but Firefighter, period.

Taco Tuesday

Tacos are another food that are greatly colored by previous experiences. Those who have experienced tacos from a street vendor in Mexico City will begrudgingly call anything else by the same name. Others that grew up with tacos being browned ground beef with salt and pepper and no other seasoning are astounded to discover the variety of flavors that can be found in tacos. Commercial taco seasoning packets are available in stores for next to nothing, but why let some corporation decide how your tacos will taste? Even if you're using the same recipe you always use, shake things up a little with the type of tortilla you use, or the toppings you make available. Cheese, sour cream, crema, lettuce, salsa, pico de gallo, guacamole, raw diced onions, olives, diced tomatoes, cilantro - add whatever you like to make even the same old, same old taco different.

Traditional Tacos

It doesn't get much more traditional than this recipe when it comes to Americanized tacos. I liked making the seasoning myself, not only because it saved me a little at the store in the morning, but I was able to have the flavor come out the way I wanted.

Taco seasoning (recipe also on page 165)
2 Tablespoons chili powder (recipe on page 160)
1 Tablespoon ground cumin
2 teaspoons salt
2 teaspoons ground black pepper
1 teaspoon paprika
$1/2$ teaspoon garlic powder
$1/2$ teaspoon onion powder
$1/2$ teaspoon crushed red pepper flakes
$1/2$ teaspoon dried oregano flakes

4 $1/2$ pounds ground chuck (80/20)
1 large sweet onion, diced
12 tortillas, soft taco size
Toppings of choice

Mix all seasoning ingredients, set aside
Brown ground chuck with the onions, drain fat
Mix seasoning with $1/2$ cup water (I use 1 Tablespoon per $1/2$ pound of meat)
Add water/seasoning mix to meat in pan
Over low flame, stirring frequently, heat until water evaporates

Korean Beef Tacos

I like to travel, and I like to visit brewpubs and drink their beer while travelling. Just outside of Burlington, VT., in a town called Williston lies Burlington Beer Company. It was heartily recommended to me that I try their Korean Beef Tacos. Looking at the description, it didn't really seem like something in my strike zone, but with how they were recommended I decided to take a swing. HOME RUN!! Immediately after returning home from the Green Mountain State I set about trying to recreate them at home. Below is my attempt at BBCO's Korean Beef Tacos with my own personalization added.

4 $^1/_2$ pounds taco meat
$^1/_2$ cup soy sauce
4 Tablespoons white sugar (or equivalent sugar substitute)
6 cloves garlic, run through garlic press
2 thumb size pieces ginger, grated
Quick pickled radishes and carrots (recipe below)
1 cucumber, diced
Sriracha sauce, or mix Sriracha and mayonnaise
Crushed peanuts
1 bunch cilantro
Wrap of choice – soft tortillas, boston bibb lettuce, etc…

Quick Pickled Radishes and Carrots

5-6 radishes, thinly sliced
5-6 ounces matchstick carrots
6 cloves garlic, run through garlic press
$^1/_2$ teaspoon crushed red pepper flakes
1 cup rice wine vinegar
1 cup water
4 Tablespoon white sugar (or equivalent sugar substitute)
1 Tablespoon and 1 teaspoon salt

Mix meat, soy sauce, sugar, garlic, and ginger in bowl, cover with plastic wrap and put in refrigerator for at least four hours

Make Quick Pickled Radishes and Carrots, refrigerate for at least 30 minutes

Preheat pot on High heat, when hot add in meat

Stir regularly, heat until all liquid is evaporated (Usually ended up being 30-40 minutes)

Serve on wrap of choice, top with radishes, carrots, cucumber, Sriracha sauce, peanuts, and cilantro

Tacos al Bomberos del Barrio

I was working at the station in the predominantly Mexican part of town (that we affectionately referred to as "La casa del Bomberos del barrio") and we ended up having to go to the specialty grocery store right down the street to get our stuff for Taco Tuesday. The specialty store didn't have ground beef for some reason, but at the meat counter they had "Taco meat." Not being familiar with it, I asked the worker how to prepare it best. He told me to mix a cup and a half of water with five packets per pound of Sazon seasoning, let marinate for a few hours, then cook it. From those basic directions, I eventually settled on the recipe below. The onion was added because when I was young, my Mom would add onion to ground beef for tacos to "stretch" the meat, and I liked the taste it contributed. The beer replaced the water because anytime you replace water with beer it makes things better! Example – a bottle of water. Seriously, the slightly sweet maltiness from the beer definitely helps elevate the flavor.

1 bottle beer, can be any beer but stay away from hoppy beers
1 $1/4$ cup homemade sazon seasoning (recipe on page 164)
4 $1/2$ pounds taco meat (available at your local ethnic grocery store, basically cubed meat as opposed to ground meat)
1 sweet onion, diced
Pinch crushed red pepper (to taste)
12 tortillas, soft taco size
Toppings of choice

Like with the meatloaf, I figured $3/4$ pound of meat per person
If using packets, use five packets of seasoning per pound of meat
If using homemade sazon, use 2 $1/2$ Tablespoons per pound of meat
Whisk seasoning into beer
Mix meat, onion, and crushed red pepper into marinade, cover with plastic wrap and put in refrigerator for at least four hours
Preheat pot on High heat, when hot add in meat
Stir regularly, heat until all liquid is evaporated (Usually ended up being 30-40 minutes)
Serve with warmed tortillas and toppings of choice

The Ladder Company

Ladder trucks take on many forms, but their mission is the same. While the goal of the Engine Firefighter is to put the wet stuff on the red stuff, the Ladder Firefighter has many other tasks to perform on a fire scene. The general duties of a Ladder company on a fire scene include: forcible entry, ventilation, search and rescue, laddering the building, salvage, shutting off the utilities, and overhaul. They may also flow water from their ladder if necessary.

Forcible entry can be as simple as kicking a door in, or as complicated as having to get through scissor gates or roll up doors, then get through locked doors. Basically, anything done to prevent those who wish to illegally enter a property must be overcome quickly, to enable access to the building and the fire within it.

Ventilation takes many forms also. They range from the type many think of, vertical ventilation (cutting a hole in the roof) to horizontal (opening or breaking windows) to recent advances in Positive Pressure Ventilation (using a high power fan to pressurize the building, then creating and/or eliminating openings to control when and where the smoke is removed). All have their time and place, and using the wrong type at the wrong time can lead to the opposite of what you are trying to accomplish, making the building safer by the removal of products of combustion.

As an Engine crew is advancing their hoseline to extinguish the fire, they are also keeping an eye out for victims, but the main job of search and rescue falls to the Ladder company. Technology has come along to help with Thermal Imaging Cameras (TIC), but if used, they need to be used as another tool in the toolbox that helps make the job easier. TICs have limitations, plus batteries can go dead at the most inopportune moment, so having the basics down cold is still important. This task falls to the Ladder company since they are unencumbered by having to drag a hoseline (making searching quicker) plus if they find a victim the firefighting can continue by the Engine company while the victim is removed.

Laddering the building helps not only the fighting of the fire, but it also gives multiple avenues to exit the building. If conditions change and a firefighter needs to exit the building RIGHT NOW, it's much easier to go to the nearest window as opposed to remembering where they are in the building and retracing their path to exit, especially if that path is compromised by the fire. The number one priority of firefighters, rescue, is also helped by laddering the building. We had our SCBA on our back with 20+ minutes of breathing air (contrary to popular belief, we had compressed air in our tanks, not oxygen) flowing into our mask – our victim we just rescued wasn't as fortunate. The quicker and easier we got them out of the building, the earlier they were able to breathe fresh air.

A function that isn't often thought of is salvage. Salvage is the protection of items in areas unaffected by the fire. Salvage can include throwing tarps over items on the floor(s) below the fire, using tarps to create a path for the overflow water to flow away from what they are trying to protect, removing items if it is easier, securing access points (boarding windows and/or doors), etc… Cities often had a separate division, most often called either the Fire Patrol or Protectives, whose entire job consisted of salvage work. Many of these were funded by the insurance companies, since they were able to reduce the amount of damage and therefore reduce the money paid out by the insurance companies. Even the biggest of cities have disbanded the separate salvage division and relegated the function to Ladder companies.

Utility control involves exactly what it sounds like, controlling or shutting off the utilities. Electric, gas (whether natural gas or propane), water, steam are all turned off for safety. Sometimes these are able to be shut off from the relative safety of the outside, but often it is necessary to go to the lowest level of the building.

Overhaul seems to be unnecessary additional damage until you understand why it is done. Before leaving the scene, we need to ensure every bit of fire is extinguished. Due to construction, sometimes fire can extend far beyond what you would normally expect. Overhaul is the exposing and dousing of any possible area where the fire could have spread to. Overhaul mainly involves removing walls and ceilings and removing household items. One single spot that is left smoldering can lead to a rekindle, which generally ends up being far worse than the original fire.

Wing Wednesday

From their humble beginnings in a Buffalo, NY. bar, Buffalo Wings have become a worldwide craze. Once thought only useful for creating chicken stock, entire restaurant chains have sprung up based on the humble wing. While a great munchie when out drinking with your buddies, it gets rather expensive to feed a bunch of hungry firefighters with the little appendages. For that reason, even though I called it Wing Wednesday, I used chicken leg quarters. If you're making actual wings, you can follow the same recipes. Not only were they less than 10% of the price, but there is so much more meat on a leg quarter compared to the same weight in wings. For six hungry firefighters, I would usually use an entire 10 pound bag of leg quarters. Even not on sale, a 10 pound bag could be had for less than $6.00. To get the protein for the meal for less than $1.00 per person really opened up options for either a more expensive other meal or being able to set aside money for a more expensive meal later. The basic recipe is the same for all of the varieties – coat with the rub (if called for), refrigerate for at least one hour, coat in the sauce, then bake at 400F for 35 minutes, flip, then bake for 15 more minutes. If you want, you can run them through the sauce again before serving.

Standard Wings

Here's the basic recipe for what started the whole craze. By choosing the hot sauce you like, these can range anywhere from mild to face melting.

1 $^1/_2$ cups all purpose flour
1 teaspoon cayenne pepper
1 teaspoon garlic powder
1 teaspoon salt
10 pounds chicken leg quarters
1 cup melted butter
1 cup hot pepper sauce of choice
1 pound baby carrots
1 bunch celery, sliced into pieces the same size as the baby carrots
Bleu cheese dressing or ranch dressing for dipping

Line baking sheet with nonstick foil, or with regular foil and spray with non-stick cooking spray
Mix flour, cayenne pepper, garlic powder, and salt
Coat chicken with mixture
Refrigerate for at least one hour
Preheat oven to 400F
Whisk melted butter and hot sauce together
Dip chicken into butter mixture and put back on sheet
Cook 35 minutes, flip, then cook for 15 more minutes, until thermometer inserted in thickest part of thigh reads 165F
Chicken can be recoated in butter mixture if desired
Serve with carrots, celery, and dressing

Grilled No-sauce Wings

I liked this version for the smokiness that not only came from grilling the chicken, but also from the spice mix. The hardest part of cooking these was the gas grills we had at the station weren't always the best quality, and weren't taken care of the best, so I had to constantly move the chicken around from hot spots to cool spots and vice versa.

1 cup brown sugar
4 Tablespoons garlic powder
2 Tablespoons chili powder (recipe on page 160)
2 Tablespoons paprika
2 Tablespoons cumin
2 Tablespoons ground black pepper
2 Tablespoons dry mustard powder
2 teaspoons cayenne pepper
2 Tablespoons salt (or to taste)
10 pounds chicken leg quarters
1 pound baby carrots
1 bunch celery, sliced into pieces the same size as the baby carrots
Bleu cheese dressing or ranch dressing for dipping

Whisk all the dry ingredients together
Coat the chicken with the rub
Refrigerate for at least one hour
Preheat grill to Medium
Grill, flipping often, until thermometer inserted in thickest part of thigh reads 165F
Serve with carrots, celery, and dressing

Teriyaki Wings

For those that don't like any spice whatsoever, but still want to do wings, this Asian inspired recipe hits the target dead in the middle.

2 cups soy sauce
2 cups white sugar
2 cups pineapple juice
$^{1}/_{2}$ cup vegetable oil
6 cloves garlic, run through garlic press
2 thumb sized pieces of ginger, grated
10 pounds chicken leg quarters
1 pound baby carrots
1 bunch celery, sliced into pieces the same size as the baby carrots
Bleu cheese dressing or ranch dressing for dipping

Whisk together soy sauce, sugar, pineapple juice, vegetable oil, garlic, and ginger
Add chicken, marinate in refrigerator at least one hour
Preheat oven to 400F
Line baking sheet with nonstick foil, or with regular foil and spray with non-stick cooking spray
Cook 35 minutes, flip, drizzle with marinade, then cook for 15 more minutes, until thermometer inserted in thickest part of thigh reads 165F
Boil remaining marinade until thickened, toss with chicken when done
Serve with carrots, celery, and dressing

Crunchy Spicy Honey Wings

Just like my sausage gravy, sometimes I like a little sweet with my heat. The crunch from the crushed cereal adds that little something extra that punches these up a notch.

4 teaspoons salt, divided
4 teaspoons ground black pepper, divided
2 teaspoons garlic powder
2 teaspoons onion powder
10 pounds chicken leg quarters
6 cups corn flakes cereal, crushed
1 cup all purpose flour
1 cup cornmeal
1 cup honey
1 teaspoon crushed red pepper flakes
1 pound baby carrots
1 bunch celery, sliced into pieces the same size as the baby carrots
Bleu cheese dressing or ranch dressing for dipping

Whisk together $^1/_2$ the salt, $^1/_2$ the pepper, garlic powder, and onion powder
Coat the chicken with the rub, refrigerate for at least one hour
Preheat oven to 400F
Line baking sheet with nonstick foil, or with regular foil and spray with non-stick cooking spray
Whisk together corn flakes, flour, cornmeal, remaining salt and pepper
Coat the chicken with the corn flake mixture and place on baking sheet
Spray top of chicken with non-stick cooking spray
Bake 35 minutes, flip, then bake 15 more minutes until thermometer inserted in thickest part of thigh reads 165F
While the chicken is cooking, stir together the honey and red pepper flakes in a small saucepan
Heat over a medium flame, stirring, until the honey thins
When chicken is done, place in large mixing bowl and coat with honey sauce
Toss until evenly coated and serve with carrots, celery, and dressing

Ladder Trucks

As mentioned before, ladder trucks come in many shapes and sizes. Each type has its own advantages and disadvantages, but they all perform the same basic tasks – get the crew and their equipment to the scene and provide a rig mounted ladder to reach beyond where ground ladders can.

Ladder trucks not only carry their main aerial ladder, but they also carry far more ground ladders than an engine would. Ladder trucks are also known as the biggest toolbox around, carrying everything from axes to forcible entry tools to gas powered saws. Departments that don't have specific salvage units often carry the salvage equipment on their ladders. If a department doesn't have a rescue squad, again, all that stuff ends up on the ladder. Because of the storage capacity, ladder trucks usually get everything that won't fit onto an engine stuffed into their compartments.

Tractor drawn aerials (TDAs or tiller trucks) are what many think of when they think of a ladder truck. TDAs are the trucks that have two steering wheels, one on the front and one in the back for guiding the trailer to follow the tractor. Their maneuverability is unmatched, as is their capacity for equipment. Unfortunately, since there is a cab on top of the truck itself for the tillerman, TDAs tend to be tall as well as long, which can affect their ability to fit into a fire station. Another drawback of a TDA is that it requires two drivers, which is often a premium position requiring paying more than a firefighter would require. TDAs fell out of favor due to their drawbacks, but recently have become more popular again due to their advantages. Due to the physics involved, the driver of the back end has to steer the opposite of what you are used to. Having driven vehicles that have a steering wheel anywhere you can possibly have one, I can tell you on a warm Summer day, with the doors of the tiller cab open, tillerman is the best job in the world!

Rear mount ladder trucks can carry the next most equipment, but still have height issues, as well as length issues when it comes to maneuverability. Rear mounts come with either a straight ladder or with a bucket at the end of the ladder. Ladder trucks with a bucket are often called either tower ladders or platforms. Just like with engines, whether a department goes with a straight stick or a bucket depends on the particular hazards they face.

Mid mount ladder trucks carry less equipment than rear mount, but their height and length are less, giving them better maneuverability. Mid mounts can also either have a straight stick or a bucket.

Another type of ladder truck is a snorkel or articulating boom platform. Conceived in Chicago by Fire Commissioner Bob Quinn, snorkels carry very little equipment, but due to how they work have advantages reaching areas where a conventional ladder cannot.

A subset of ladder trucks are called "Quints." Quints are called such because there are five main functions of fire vehicles: carry water, carry hose, ability to pump water, carry ground ladders, and have a truck mounted aerial device. Traditionally, engines, or triple combination pumpers take care of the first three functions while ladders cover the last two. A quint has all five functions. Quints can come in any of the same forms that any other ladder is available in.

Tot Waffle Thursday

Tot waffles are just what they sound like – waffles made from tater tots. You can thaw tater tots and then run them through a waffle iron, but I preferred buying the preformed hash brown patties like you can get deep fried from fast food restaurants and running them through the waffle iron. Very few have enough waffle irons to cook up enough tot waffles to feed the whole crew at once, so if you have a baking sheet in a 170F oven, you can do multiple batches and keep the early ones warm without overcooking them. You can just bake the hash brown patties, but when you run them through the waffle iron you create nice little pockets to help hold the sauce or toppings in place.

Full Throttle Tot Waffle

Rochester, NY., has their Garbage Plate (home fries, macaroni salad, baked beans, topped with meat of choice and spicy meat sauce), Springfield, IL. has their Horseshoe (Texas toast, meat of choice, cheese sauce, and french fries) – I wanted to come up with my own concoction. You can make a mornay sauce if you prefer, but every time I tried to at the station getting interrupted by an emergency call would ruin it, whereas a pasteurized prepared cheese product is much more forgiving.

Pulled pork (recipe on page 142)
1 box (15) preformed hash brown patties, defrosted
Cole slaw (recipe on page 79)
8 ounce block pasteurized prepared cheese product
2 ounces precooked, crumbled bacon
Beer to taste, can be any beer but stay away from hoppy beers
16 ounces sour cream

Make pulled pork, take hash brown patties out of freezer and defrost on counter
Make cole slaw, cover and refrigerate for at least two hours
Cook hash brown patties
Melt pasteurized prepared cheese product in small saucepan or microwave
Mix in the bacon, then the beer

To serve, place a waffle (or two) on plate
Cover with beer bacon cheese sauce
Cover with sour cream
Cover with pulled pork
Top with cole slaw

Breakfast Tot Waffle

Who doesn't like breakfast for supper? You can cook the eggs however you prefer, scrambled, over easy, sunny side up, poached…it's all good! Wait until just before serving to add the pepper. The longer the pepper sits in the gravy, the hotter it will get, taking a just right gravy to way too hot without realizing it until the first bite.

1 box (15) preformed hash brown patties, defrosted
2 pounds maple breakfast sausage
$^{1}/_{2}$ large sweet onion, diced
$^{1}/_{2}$ cup all purpose flour
4 cups whole milk
Pinch each of salt, black pepper, and crushed red pepper to taste
Extra large eggs (one per waffle if over easy or sunny side up, 18 if scrambling)

At least four hours prior to cooking, thaw hash brown patties on counter
Cook hash brown patties
Brown sausage and onion in large pot
Stir in flour until fully mixed
Gradually stir in milk
Cook gravy until thickness is what you like
Cook eggs
Season gravy to taste

To serve, if using scrambled eggs, top tot waffles with eggs, then cover with gravy. If using any other form of eggs, top tot waffles with gravy, then place egg on top

Chili Mac & Cheese Tot Waffle

Chili? What better to have at the Firehouse? Mac and cheese? Who doesn't like mac and cheese? Mac and cheese covered with chili on a tot waffle? No hip checks allowed as the family rushes to the table! Instead of two minutes in the penalty box, any violations mean that person is last to get their food.

1 box (15) preformed hash brown patties, defrosted
Chili of choice (recipes start on page 106)
8 ounces dry pasta of choice (I always kinda liked cavatappi)
8 ounce block pasteurized prepared cheese product
beer to taste, can be any beer but stay away from hoppy beers
Chili toppings

At least four hours prior to cooking, thaw hash brown patties on counter
Cook hash brown patties
Put your pasta in a pot
Cover with salted water, bring to a boil
Stir, turn off the heat, and cover
Melt pasteurized prepared cheese product in small saucepan or microwave
Mix in beer to taste
After 10 minutes, check if the pasta is done to your liking
Drain pasta, mix cheese sauce in

To serve, top tot waffles with mac and cheese, then cover with chili and whatever chili toppings you prefer

Loco Moco Tot Waffle

Many a morning in Hawaii starts off with Loco Moco. I simply replaced the traditional sticky white rice with a tot waffle and boom! Loco Moco tot waffle!

1 box (15) preformed hash brown patties, defrosted
1 $^1/_2$ pounds ground chuck (80/20)
salt to taste
Ground black pepper to taste
1 medium sliced sweet onion
$^3/_4$ cup beef broth
$^1/_2$ pound sliced mushrooms
1 $^1/_2$ (12 ounces each) jars brown gravy
6 eggs

At least four hours prior to cooking, thaw hash brown patties on counter
Cook hash brown patties
Coat cast iron skillet(s) with non-stick cooking spray and heat over medium heat
Divide beef into 6 equal portions, form into patties
Salt and pepper patties well
Fry patties to medium (140F)
Remove patties to plate, leaving drippings in skillet(s)
Stir onion and beef broth into drippings, reduce heat to low
Cook until onions are slightly soft, add mushrooms to skillet(s)
Cook until onions and mushrooms are soft
Pour gravy over onions and mushrooms, stir and cook until hot
Put patties in gravy, simmer until patties are reheated
Cook eggs sunny side up

To serve, place a beef patty on each hash brown patty, cover with gravy, then top it off with an egg

Buffalo Chicken Tot Waffle

When eating Buffalo wings, I normally don't eat the carrots and celery, but with them shredded and sliced VERY thin, they certainly add texture and a little cool to mingle with the heat of the dry ingredients and sauce.

6 preformed hash brown patties, defrosted
$^1/_2$ cup brown sugar
2 Tablespoons garlic powder
1 Tablespoon chili powder (see recipe on page 160)
1 Tablespoon paprika
1 Tablespoon cumin
1 Tablespoon dry mustard powder
1 Tablespoon ground black pepper
1 teaspoon cayenne pepper
2 Tablespoons salt (or to taste)
3 boneless skinless chicken breasts
$^1/_2$ cup melted butter
$^1/_2$ cup hot pepper sauce
2 carrots, shredded
2 stalks celery, sliced thinly
Bleu cheese dressing or ranch dressing for drizzling

At least four hours prior to cooking, thaw hash brown patties on counter
Whisk all the dry ingredients together
Pound chicken to $^1/_2$" thick, cut in half so pieces are same size as hash brown patties
Coat with dry ingredient mix, refrigerate for at least one hour
Cook hash brown patties
Coat chicken with butter mixture
Cook chicken on medium-hot grill, flipping often until 165F internally
If desired, coat chicken with butter mixture again after cooking

To serve, place a chicken breast on each hash brown patty, drizzle dressing over chicken, then garnish with carrots and celery

Tenders

A tender (sometimes referred to as a tanker) is used to transport large volumes of water to areas that do not have an established water supply system. In the United States, a vehicle must carry a minimum of 1,000 gallons of water to be considered a tender. Some tractor/trailer tenders can carry upwards of 8,000 gallons! That water must come from somewhere, which can be a lake, a stream, a dry hydrant, a cistern, or even a pressurized hydrant that's too far away to lay supply hose from. Unless it's hooked up to a pressurized hydrant, a tender must "draft" the water from the source through a semi rigid hose that won't collapse under the suction required. This is accomplished by creating a partial vacuum in a pump and letting atmospheric pressure push the water into the pump, much like sucking on a straw. Being limited by how much atmospheric pressure can push on the source, the theoretical maximum height that water can be drafted from is 33.9 feet. In reality, 30 feet is the general maximum lift.

Just like engines and ladders, tenders are customized to their specific needs, leading to a wide variety not just nationwide but even from station to station within the same department. Some have a small pump only used for drafting water from whatever source they can find, others have a larger pump able to draft and to push water faster to where it's supplying, while others are set up like a full fledged engine that just happens to have a large tank and can act as a tender.

One the water is obtained, circumstances determine the method used to get it to the engine pumping at a fire scene. On a scene with limited access and a tender equipped with a pump large enough, a supply hose can go directly from the tender to the engine. If the distance is too great or the tender doesn't have a suitable pump, water can be drafted and transported closer to the fire scene, dumped into a portable tank, then drafted by an engine and pumped to the fire scene. When scene access is not a concern, water can be drafted and transported to a tank next to the engine on scene, which can draft the water it needs directly from the portable tank.

Fish Friday

Eating fish on Fridays started as a loophole around the early Christian requirement of fasting on Fridays in memory of Christ's death. Originally, adult church members were called upon to abstain from meat on all Fridays and also Wednesdays during Lent. The church didn't specifically call for eating fish, but when told to avoid eating warm blooded land animals, why not eat cold blooded sea animals?

Mass immigration during the Industrial Revolution helped to spread the tradition of eating fish on Fridays. Many immigrants to the United States came from Catholic countries and eventually settled in the interior of the country. With the advent of refrigeration, these people far from the ocean were able to get "fresh" fish, which greatly increased the demand. To this day, Friday fish fries are so popular in Wisconsin, pretty much every restaurant in the state must have one or risk having an empty building on Friday nights. I once ate lunch with my wife at a Mexican restaurant in Wisconsin and was humorously surprised to see a table tent advertising their Friday fish fry!

Two subjects sure to raise the temperature in a fire station are politics and religion, yet tradition makes Fish Friday somehow non-religious. I have enjoyed fried fish at the station many times, however the aroma left behind tends to last all through the next two days, leading to the other two shifts not being thrilled with the cook. Due to the staying power of the fried fish aroma, I generally stuck to baking it and trying to get it as close to fried as possible. You can use whatever type of fish you prefer with whichever recipe you like I included the type I would usually use for each recipe.

Baked Panko Cod

What is panko, anyway? Because of the way it's made, panko has a dryer, flakier consistency, which absorbs less oil. Because it absorbs less oil, it ends up lighter and crunchier than regular bread crumbs.

6 cod fillets
1 $^1/_2$ cups panko bread crumbs
3 teaspoon dried dill, divided
$^1/_3$ cup mayonnaise
1 Tablespoon and 1 $^1/_2$ teaspoon dijon mustard
1 Tablespoon and 1 $^1/_2$ teaspoon fresh lemon juice
Pinch of salt and ground black pepper (to taste)
Wedges of lemon for serving
Tartar sauce for serving (recipe on page 166)

Preheat oven to 450F
Toss panko bread crumbs with half of the dill
In separate bowl, mix remaining dill, mayonnaise, mustard, and lemon juice
Pat cod dry with paper towels, season with salt and pepper
Lay cod on baking sheet sprayed with non-stick cooking spray
Brush tops and sides of cod with mayonnaise mixture
Sprinkle and press bread crumb mixture onto mayonnaise covered cod
Lightly spray cod with non-stick cooking spray
Bake on middle rack until crumbs are golden brown and fish flakes easily, about 15 minutes
Serve with lemon wedges and tartar sauce

Baked Parmesan Tilapia

Tilapia is a rather plain tasting fish, which really benefits from the array of spices mixed in with the bread crumbs.

$^1/_2$ cup milk
$^1/_2$ cup ranch dressing
$^1/_2$ cup all purpose flour
1 cup seasoned bread crumbs
$^1/_2$ cup grated parmesan cheese
$^1/_2$ teaspoon season salt
$^1/_2$ teaspoon ground black pepper
$^1/_2$ teaspoon celery salt
$^1/_2$ teaspoon garlic powder
$^1/_2$ teaspoon onion powder
$^1/_2$ teaspoon paprika
$^1/_2$ teaspoon dried parsley
6 (6 ounces each) tilapia fillets
Wedges of lemon for serving
Tartar sauce for serving (recipe on page 166)

Mix milk and dressing in shallow bowl big enough to fit largest piece of fish
Place flour in similar bowl
Whisk together all dry ingredients
Spray bread crumb mixture with non-stick cooking spray until damp, then whisk
Repeat until crumb mixture is lightly moistened
Preheat oven to 425F
Line baking sheet with foil, then spray with non-stick cooking spray
Coat fish with flour, shaking off excess
Dip fish into milk/dressing mixture
Coat with bread crumb mixture and place on baking sheet
Spray fish lightly with non-stick cooking spray
Bake until fish flakes easily, 20-25 minutes
Serve with lemon wedges and tartar sauce

Oven Fried Catfish

Catfish and cornmeal go together like peanut butter and jelly. The sweet flavor of the catfish is complemented very well by the lightly spicy crunch of the cornmeal breading. Soaking it in milk for 20 minutes before cooking helps "clean" the flavor of the catfish.

3 pounds catfish fillets
1 cup yellow cornmeal
2 teaspoons paprika
2 teaspoons dried thyme
2 teaspoons salt
1 teaspoon celery seed
1 teaspoon onion powder
1 teaspoon garlic powder
1 teaspoon ground black pepper
1 cup milk
Wedges of lemon for serving
Tartar sauce for serving (recipe on page 166)

Preheat oven to 425F
Line a baking sheet with foil and coat with non-stick cooking spray
Whisk together all dry ingredients in shallow bowl big enough to fit largest piece of fish
Pour milk into similar bowl
Dry fish with paper towels
Dip fish into milk
Place fish in cornmeal mixture and coat liberally
Place fish on baking sheet
Coat tops of fish with non-stick cooking spray until moist
Bake until fish flakes easily, about 15 minutes
Serve with lemon wedges and tartar sauce

Easy Shrimp Fettucine Alfredo

No, this isn't a traditional alfredo, but just like the mornay for Mac and Cheese, if I tried to make the traditional we always caught a run and ruined the sauce. This recipe is extremely versatile – you can use any pasta you prefer, broccoli florets instead of peas, chicken or scallops instead of shrimp, Cajun seasoning instead of black pepper, etc... If you're not the mushroom type, don't worry, you won't even notice them in the finished dish. If just the thought of mushrooms being involved is a deal breaker, you can use Cream of Shrimp soup, your sauce will just end up pinkish. If the same applies and you're using chicken as your protein, you can use Cream of Chicken soup and your sauce will be yellowish, but still taste fine.

1 $^1/_2$ (16 ounces each) packages fettucine
1 $^1/_2$ (12 ounces each) packages frozen peas
1 stick plus 2 Tablespoons salted butter
3 pounds frozen, de-veined, tail off cooked shrimp (whatever count per pound you prefer)
3 (10.75 ounces each) cans cream of mushroom soup (or one 22.6 ounce and one 10.75 ounce)
1 $^1/_2$ cups milk
1 $^1/_4$ cup parmesan cheese
Ground black pepper to taste, start with $^3/_4$ teaspoon

Cook pasta according to package directions, adding vegetables last 3-4 minutes
Drain pasta/veggie mix
Heat butter in skillet
Cook shrimp until opaque, stirring often
Add soup, milk, cheese, black pepper, and pasta/veggie mixture
Heat through, stirring often
Serve with additional parmesan cheese

Fajita Friday

Yes, there are some people out there that absolutely, under any circumstance, will not eat seafood. Yes, they're out there, and other than their aversion to seafood can be fine human beings. Given that our shift schedule was 24 hours on followed by 48 hours off, that meant Fajita Friday was the workday that immediately followed Taco Tuesday. Even though department wise it was the next day, since there was two real life days in between no one seemed to mind Mexican two workdays in a row.

Here in Northern Illinois the weather mandated having versions I could do indoors, even though on the grill was my favorite way to cook fajitas. For any of the recipes, you can use your protein of choice – chicken, steak, shrimp (if you're not doing Fajita Friday to avoid Fish Friday) – whatever your heart desires.

The toppings you serve with your fajitas are up to you as well. The same toppings that go with tacos go well with fajitas. How you soften your tortillas is up to you also. Some prefer heating them directly over an open flame, some like in a cast iron pan, while for others a microwave fills the bill. As long as it does what you're trying to accomplish, rock on!

Grilled Fajitas

Conventional fajitas rock, but I always liked the extra oomph from cooking them on a grill. As with any time you cook boneless skinless chicken breasts, take care not to overcook them. Feel free to poke them with a thermometer, because even though some juice escapes, it'll dry out much less from that than overcooking it.

4 pounds boneless skinless chicken breast
3 Tablespoons corn starch
2 Tablespoons chili powder (recipe on page 160)
1 Tablespoon paprika
1 Tablespoon salt
1 Tablespoon white sugar
1 $^1/_2$ teaspoon ground cumin
1 $^1/_2$ teaspoon garlic powder
1 $^1/_2$ teaspoon onion powder
$^3/_4$ teaspoon cayenne pepper
2 medium sweet onions, sliced
4 bell peppers, color of choice, sliced
$^1/_2$ stick salted butter, divided
12 tortillas
Toppings for fajitas

Pound chicken breasts to $^1/_2$" thick
Mix all dry ingredients in bowl
Coat chicken breasts with mixture, refrigerate for at least one hour
Preheat grill to Medium-High, leaving one section on Low
Make foil pouches for onions and peppers
Sprinkle seasoning over onions and peppers
Place pats of butter over onions and peppers
Close pouches and place on low section of grill
Cook chicken on medium-hot section, flipping often until 150F internally
Let chicken rest for 3 minutes, slice into strips
Pull onions and peppers off grill when soft
Serve with warmed tortillas, onions and peppers, and toppings of choice

Sheet Pan Chicken Fajitas

These are great when the weather's cold outside and you have a crowd to feed (The Big Game to end the season?). It's easy to ramp up as far as size of the dish without having to do too much more prep, and the cooking is exactly the same whether for 6 (recipe below) or 16!

$^1/_2$ cup vegetable oil
2 Tablespoons chili powder (recipe on page 160)
1 Tablespoon paprika
1 Tablespoon salt
1 Tablespoon white sugar
1 $^1/_2$ teaspoons ground cumin
1 $^1/_2$ teaspoon garlic powder
1 $^1/_2$ teaspoon onion powder
$^3/_4$ teaspoon cayenne pepper
4 pounds boneless skinless chicken breast, sliced
2 medium sweet onions, sliced
4 bell peppers, color of choice, sliced
2 bunches fresh cilantro, chopped
Juice of 1 lime
Tortillas of choice
Toppings of choice

Combine vegetable oil and all spices in resealable plastic bag
Add chicken, onions, and peppers to bag, shake to mix
Marinate in refrigerator for at least two hours
Preheat oven to 400F
Line baking sheet with aluminum foil, spray with non-stick cooking spray
Spread chicken mixture on pan
Cook 10 minutes, stir
Continue cooking until chicken is done and peppers are soft, usually another 10 minutes
Sprinkle with cilantro and squeeze lime juice over chicken
Serve with warmed tortillas and toppings of choice

Hydrants

Nearly ubiquitous in urban and suburban America, most civilians only know what hydrants do thanks to movies and TV. The most obvious attribute of hydrants is that when you open them up, you get nearly unlimited water. The volume of water is important, but the pressure of that water is just as important. The more pressure, the more volume you can extract from the water system. How many times have you seen or participated in a makeshift sprinkler from a hydrant on the corner on a hot summer day? Believe it or not, that can greatly reduce the amount of water available for fighting a fire. Even a large number of people taking showers first thing in the morning can affect the pressure and volume available. Yes, hydrants are hooked into the very same water system that provides the water to your house. There are basically three types of hydrants – dry barrel, wet barrel, and dry hydrants. Dry barrel and wet barrel hydrants are both connected to a pressurized water supply system, while dry hydrants are connected to non-pressurized water supplies, such as lakes, ponds, or cisterns. While not universally used, there is a standard that addresses the color of hydrants. It is recommended that the body of hydrants are painted a high visibility color, such as chrome yellow. Some are painted with reflective paint, while others may be painted with luminescent paint. It is also recommended that the bonnet (top) and the caps are color coded according to amount of water flow expected, ranging in order of flow volume from red to orange to green to light blue.

Dry barrel hydrants are found anywhere the temperatures get below freezing on a regular basis. They are installed directly to an underground water main, with the valve that holds the water back located in the ground and a drain that allows the water to flow back out of the hydrant after use. This accomplishes two goals – the hydrant barrel itself cannot freeze, and if the hydrant is knocked off water will not come out. A disadvantage is that there is only one way to turn the flow on or off, so if you're already connected to a hydrant and flowing water, you are unable to connect another supply line to connect to another apparatus.

Wet barrel hydrants are only found where temperatures are generally warmer, since the valve that holds the water back is located in the barrel of the hydrant itself. This means that there is always water in the barrel of the hydrant. An easy way to tell if a hydrant is a dry barrel or wet barrel is by looking at the barrel itself. Dry barrel hydrants will only have one nut on the top of the hydrant to turn the hydrant on, while wet barrel hydrants will have nuts directly across from each discharge. This allows hoses to be connected to go to other apparatus after one apparatus is already connected and flowing water. When you see a vehicle hit a hydrant and water comes shooting out of the ground, that's a wet barrel hydrant.

Dry hydrants are completely different from dry barrel hydrants. In rural areas where there is not an established water supply system, dry hydrants may be installed to ease the process of drafting water for fighting a fire. Dry hydrants are installed by permanently connecting piping to a static water supply. Dry hydrants may be directly connected to by the Engine directly pumping the hoselines at a fire, but more often they are used by Tenders to fill up and bring the water to the fire scene where a portable drafting system is set up using collapsible tanks.

Whichever system is used, the firefighter at the business end of the attack line only cares that there is a sufficient amount of water to keep them safe and extinguish the fire. This requires not just the proper amount of pressure and volume of water, but a competent Engineer at the pump panel of the Engine to accept and provide the proper amount and pressure of water to that firefighter, since neither a limp hoseline or one that has too much pressure to be controlled is useful.

Pizza Saturday

On average, Americans eat 100 acres worth of pizza daily, equaling approximately 350 slices per second, 24/7/365. This puts the amount of pizza eaten right up there with how many hot dogs and hamburgers are wolfed down daily. What better comfort food to celebrate a Saturday at the fire station?

Next question is what style? Neapolitan, Sicilian, New York, New Haven, Detroit, Chicago deep dish, Chicago tavern style, Stuffed, Saint Louis, California... Entire cookbooks have been dedicated to pizza recipes, so I'll stick to the types I made at the station. While Neapolitan may be an incredible pizza, most fire stations (and homes) don't have a brick oven that reaches 900F. Likewise a coal fired oven like one that produces a New York slice. You can buy special deep dish pans or you can use 9" x 13" pans for doing deep dish, you can buy pizza pans or baking sheets for creating thin crust, hey – there's no such thing as bad pizza!

Riles' Deep Dish Pizza

Pizzeria Uno and Due, Lou Malnati's, Gino's East, Pequod's, Pizano's, there's dozens of deep dish places in Chicago and the suburbs. Which one is the best? Ask any number of people and you're likely to get just as many answers. After decades of practice, here's the recipe I settled on. This will provide enough dough for two 14" round pans or three 9" x 13" pans. If you're not using all of the dough, freeze what you're not using – it seems to come out better after freezing and thawing! This recipe also provides for pre-meal snacks for the cook. Not only did I end up with leftover pepperoni after topping one of the pizzas, but I usually bought a couple extra mushrooms. A very simple, yet delicious snack can be made just by cutting a mushroom in half and putting ranch dressing on the halves.

12 ounces malty beer, such as bock or wheat, about 100F
1 packet yeast
1 Tablespoon white sugar
4 cups all purpose flour
$^1/_2$ cup butter flavor vegetable shortening
1 teaspoon salt
3 boxes (750 grams, 26.46 ounces each) Pomi® chopped tomatoes, drained
2 pounds fresh mozzarella cheese slices, divided
2 pounds sweet Italian sausage, divided
Any other pizza toppings you desire
Dusting of parmesan cheese

Mix beer, yeast, and sugar in bowl, let proof until it foams
Mix flour, shortening, salt, and beer/yeast mixture
Knead 8-10 minutes, adding flour as necessary
Turn out into oiled bowl, cover with plastic wrap and towel
Let rise until doubled in size, usually at least one hour
Preheat oven to 450F for at least one hour
Drain tomatoes in large colander in sink
Place plastic wrap in pans, push sausage into a patty (tomato on your hands will help keep the sausage from sticking)
Remove plastic wrap and sausage from pan, hold on table until needed
Oil pans with corn oil or softened butter
Push dough in pans and pull thin outer crust up sides

Lay out mozzarella on dough
Lay sausage on top of cheese
Spread other ingredients on sausage
Spread drained tomatoes on top of all toppings
Sprinkle parmesan on top of pizzas
Place pizzas directly on oven floor for five minutes
Bake 25-30 minutes, rotating halfway through if oven is not convection
Let sit on counter for five minutes before cutting
Slice and enjoy!

Thin Crust Pizza

Even the most die hard Chicagoan doesn't eat deep dish pizza all the time. The tavern style thin crust prevalent in the multitude of bars that don't even have a name other than Old Style or Budweiser over their door is the type of pizza most eaten in Chicago. With a thin, cracker type crust, and always cut into squares (tavern cut, in the Chicago version of English), this is the stuff of many long nights spent drinking lagers chilled almost to the freezing point.

12 ounces malty beer, such as bock or wheat, about 100F
1 packet yeast
1 Tablespoon white sugar
4 cups all purpose flour
1 teaspoon salt
1 can (28 ounces) all purpose ground tomatoes
1 pound sweet Italian sausage (if desired)
Pizza toppings of choice
Shredded mozzarella (1 cup for cookie sheet, 2 cups for half baking sheet)
Oregano to sprinkle over cheese

Mix beer, yeast, and sugar in bowl, let proof until it foams
Mix flour, salt, and beer/yeast mixture
Knead 8-10 minutes, adding flour as necessary
Turn out into oiled bowl, cover with plastic wrap and towel
Let rise until doubled in size, usually at least one hour
Preheat oven to 450F
Roll dough flat, lay into pan
Spread crushed tomatoes on dough, leaving small area of crust uncovered on edges
Spread toppings evenly
Spread cheese evenly over toppings
Sprinkle oregano lightly over cheese
Bake 20 minutes, rotating halfway through if oven is not convection
Let sit on counter for five minutes before cutting
Slice (into squares) and enjoy!

Quick and Easy Calzones

Sometimes you need to make a quick pizza type dinner, and you don't have time to make your own dough. Store bought pizza dough can be difficult to spread out on a pan, but refrigerated crescent rolls happen to be the right shape and size for quick calzones. This recipes makes 12 small calzones, enough for six hungry firefighters.

3 cans (8 ounces each) refrigerated crescent rolls
3 cans (8 ounces each) pizza sauce, divided
2 cups shredded mozzarella cheese
Pizza toppings of choice (precooked if necessary)
Sprinkle of parmesan cheese over completed calzones

Preheat oven to 375F
Unroll dough and separate into rectangles
Press rectangles into approximately 6" x 4" rectangles
Firmly press perforations to seal
Spread pizza sauce on half of rectangles to within 1" of edge
Sprinkle each with cheese
Spread toppings thinly on cheese
Fold rectangles over toppings
Press edges with a fork to seal
Make small slice on top of each calzone to release steam
Bake 15 minutes, then flip and cook until golden brown, about 5 more minutes
Sprinkle parmesan cheese over calzones
Serve with remaining pizza sauce for dipping

Ambulances

At its most basic, an ambulance is any vehicle that transports sick and/or injured people for emergency or non-emergency purposes. This includes anything from a modified golf cart all the way up to an airplane. When it comes to the fire service in the United States, an ambulance is most often pickup, van, or truck based and most often used for emergency transport.

Ambulances are known by many names across the US, from a bus, to a meat wagon, ambo, or box. The bus term came from the early days of public health service where each hospital had a bus that would roam the city and anyone that needed to go to the hospital would get on the bus belonging to their hospital of choice. Meat wagon goes back to the days of ambulances being converted cars, often acting as hearses when not in use as ambulances.

Originally ambulances referred to mobile hospitals that followed armies as they went to battle, aiming to reduce fatalities by reducing the time between injury and medical care. In the 15th century, vehicles started to be used to transport the injured, and the 19th century saw the same concept applied to civilian populations. In the mid 20th century, the use of ambulances grew tremendously, but there were no standards for either the vehicles or the training required to function in them. In 1970 Los Angeles County's Freeman Memorial Hospital started the nation's first nationally accredited Paramedic program, while in 1976 the General Services Administration published its first standards for ambulances.

Today's ambulances are equipped and staffed like never before, with the ability to bring the Emergency Department directly to the patient. Defibrillators, advanced airway equipment, medications – all lead to modern ambulance crews being able to start the treatment continued in the hospital, not just scream across town in an effort to get the patient to the hospital as fast as possible. One thing that makes Paramedics different from all other health care professions is that anything they are able to do must be accomplished while the ambulance is moving.

Appetizers

Appetizers weren't a staple around the station, but on special days (holidays, big games, etc…) I liked to have either steaks or prime rib for our noon meal and then have everyone bring in an appetizer to share for the evening meal. The only down side to that plan was the times when multiple people needed the same piece of kitchen equipment at the same time. It never ended up being that big of a deal, because we just put all the appetizers out for everyone to graze at their leisure, so it didn't matter if one item ended up ready 20 minutes after everything else.

It wasn't unusual for two people to bring in similar appetizers, but only one time did two people bring in the exact same dish. It didn't matter, though, because before everybody called it a night and hit the rack every bit of food was gone.

Bacon Wrapped Jalapeno Poppers

In spite of being mostly made of jalapeno peppers, these don't end up being spicy since you remove the ribs before cooking. If you like them spicier, by all means keep the ribs, just remove the seeds.

$^1/_2$ cup cream cheese
$^1/_2$ cup sharp cheddar cheese, shredded
12 jalapeno peppers, cut in half lengthwise, ribs and seeds removed
12 slices bacon

Preheat oven to 400F
Line baking sheet with non-stick foil or regular foil sprayed with non-stick cooking spray
Mix cream cheese and cheddar cheese
Fill each jalapeno half with cheese mixture
Put halves back together
Wrap each jalapeno with a slice of bacon
Bake until bacon is crispy, around 15 minutes

Baked Oven Fried Pickles

Even people that don't like dill pickles like fried pickles! The problem with making traditional fried pickles is that you need to deep fry them. The problem at the station or at home is any deep fryer you may have will only hold a few items at once without dropping the temperature and making the food soggy with grease instead of crunchy. Some keys to this recipe include: dry the pickles well before coating by spreading out on paper towels and patting the tops dry so the coating sticks; whip the egg white for at least five minutes until it's fluffy and dry looking; shake gently in the bag so the pickle slices all get coated evenly; and don't be afraid of the olive oil. Adapted from Megan Splawn's recipe on thekitchn.com.

1 (16 ounce) jar sliced dill pickles
$^1/_2$ cup yellow cornmeal
$^1/_3$ cup all purpose flour
$^1/_2$ teaspoon cajun seasoning (recipe on page 159)
1 extra large egg white
$^1/_4$ cup olive oil
Dip of choice (ranch dressing mixed with cajun seasoning or not, fry dip, etc…)

Preheat oven to 425F with rimmed baking sheet on middle rack
Drain pickles and dry well
Mix the cornmeal, flour, and creole seasoning in a zip top bag
Whisk the egg white in a medium mixing bowl
Coat the pickle slices in the egg white by gently stirring in mixing bowl
Add pickle slices to mixing bag, shake gently to coat
Pull baking sheet from oven, pour olive oil on baking sheet
Lay pickle slices on baking sheet in single layer
Bake until golden brown and crisp, 10-12 minutes
Serve pickles hot from the oven with dip of choice

Baked Party Sandwiches

These sandwiches can be made with any variety of lunch meat and cheese. I have made or had these using ham and swiss, roast beef and bleu, turkey and cheddar… Use your imagination, just make sure the flavors meld together well.

$^3/_4$ cup melted butter
1 $^1/_2$ Tablespoons Dijon mustard
1 $^1/_2$ Tablespoons poppy seeds
1 Tablespoon dried minced onion
1 $^1/_2$ teaspoons worcestershire sauce
24 mini dinner rolls
1 pound thinly sliced lunch meat, divided
1 pound thinly sliced cheese

Preheat oven to 350F
Grease 9" x 13" baking dish
Mix butter, mustard, poppy seeds, onion, and worcestershire sauce
Separate tops from bottoms of rolls
Place bottoms of rolls in baking dish
Layer half of the lunch meat onto bottoms of rolls
Layer cheese on top of lunch meat
Top with remaining lunch meat
Place tops of rolls on sandwiches
Pour butter mixture evenly over rolls
Bake until rolls are lightly browned and cheese has melted, around 20 minutes
Slice into individual sandwiches through the meat and cheese layers

Buffalo Chicken Dip

This highly addictive dip is easy to throw together and stores well, allowing you to prepare long before needed and reheat just before serving.

2 boneless, skinless chicken breasts, cooked and shredded
$^3/_4$ cup hot sauce of choice (Frank's is traditional)
2 (8 ounces each) packages cream cheese, softened
1 cup ranch dressing
1 $^1/_2$ cups cheddar cheese, shredded, divided
1 bunch celery, cut into 4" pieces
1 box chicken flavored crackers

Over medium heat, mix chicken and hot sauce in a skillet
Once heated through, stir in cream cheese and ranch dressing
Cook, stirring until blended and warmed through
Stir in half the cheese
Transfer to slow cooker
Sprinkle remaining cheese on top
Cover, cook on low until hot and bubbly
Set slow cooker to warm setting, serve with celery and crackers

Bruschetta with Caramelized Tomatoes

Most of the recipes in this cookbook I either came up with on my own or gathered from other firefighters, and Lord help me if I can remember which recipe I got from which firefighter. This recipe I got from our dear friend Sharon Sima, who found it on the Williams-Sonoma website. I usually caramelize the tomatoes ahead of time and refrigerate until needed, which requires putting the bruschetta back in the oven after building to warm the tomatoes back up.

$1/4$ cup extra virgin olive oil
2 garlic cloves, run through garlic press
1 Tablespoon fennel seeds, coarsely pounded or crushed
Ground black pepper to taste
1 $1/2$ pounds cherry tomatoes, halved
$1/2$ teaspoon salt
Crusty French bread, cut into 3/8" slices
Extra virgin olive oil for brushing bread
1 (8 ounce) tub ricotta cheese
1 package (0.75 ounce) fresh basil, chiffonade cut

Stir together olive oil, garlic, fennel seeds, and pepper
Let stand for 30 minutes
Preheat oven to 300F
Arrange tomatoes cut side up on rimmed baking sheet
Drizzle olive oil mixture over tomatoes, then sprinkle salt over tomatoes
Bake until tomatoes are partially shriveled, around 1 $1/2$ hours
Transfer tomatoes to a bowl, making sure to get juices and browned bits
Turn broiler on in oven with top rack about 4" below flame
Brush bread slices with olive oil
Arrange on baking sheet, broil until edges are lightly browned, 1-2 minutes
Spread a heaping Tablespoon of ricotta on each slice of bread
Top with a heaping Tablespoon of tomatoes, then top with basil
Return to oven if necessary, then serve and enjoy!

Caprese Salad

As with most classic recipes, there is no one true history of its conception. Caprese Salad first made an appearance on a print menu in the 1920's, while it did not become widespread until the 1950's. Simple, easy to put together, yet nothing better with happy hour when the weather turns hot outside. Make sure your tomatoes are ripe – not ripe yet and the tomatoes are "bony," overripe and they end up mushy and don't hold their shape when you pick them up off the serving platter. Until someone figures out a way to grow bacon in a garden, Roma tomatoes fresh from the garden for this salad is the best reason for a garden, in my humble opinion. If you can't find balsamic reduction at your local grocery store, just mix 1 cup balsamic vinegar with $1/4$ cup honey. Bring to a boil in a small saucepan, then reduce the heat to low and simmer until the mixture has reduced to about $1/3$ cup. Make sure to allow the mixture to cool before using on your salad.

3 Roma tomatoes, cut widthwise into $3/8$" slices
1 (16 ounce) package fresh mozzarella cheese slices
Pinch of salt to taste
Fresh ground black pepper to taste
1 package (0.75 ounce) fresh basil
$1/4$ cup extra virgin olive oil
Drizzle of balsamic reduction

Lay tomatoes on serving platter
Lay a mozzarella slice on top of each tomato slice
Sprinkle with salt and pepper to taste (less is more)
Tear basil leaves off by hand, lay on top of each slice of mozzarella
Drizzle with olive oil and balsamic reduction (again – less is more)
Let warm on countertop for at least 15 minutes before serving

Corn Caprese Salad

When I was at stations that had gardens, whoever was in charge of the garden would usually plant a variety of tomatoes, including cherry and/or grape tomatoes. In the sort of making lemonade out of lemons serendipity, I had brought fresh mozzarella to make Caprese Salad counting on getting the tomatoes and basil from our garden. We didn't have any Roma tomatoes ripe, but we had a bunch of grape tomatoes that were. We also had quite a bit of corn on the cob left over from the previous day's shift. Not wanting to waste the mozzarella, I cut it into small pieces, cut the leftover corn off the cobs, cut the grape tomatoes in half, and created this recipe. Over the years I've modified it slightly into a taste and texture my wife and I can agree on, which is the version below. The best method I have found to cook the corn is similar to the one I use for pasta - shuck it, put it in boiling water, shut off heat, cover, and let sit for 10 minutes. If desired, you can add 2 Tablespoons of sugar and/or the juice of one lemon into the water. When cutting off the cob, make sure to let the corn cool first.

4 ears corn on the cob
1 pound grape tomatoes, halved
1 pound fresh mozzarella cheese, cubed, or 1 pound fresh mozzarella pearls
3 lemons, zested then juiced
Pinch of salt to taste
Ground black pepper to taste
1 package (0.75 ounce) fresh basil, chiffonade cut

Cook, then chill corn on the cob
Cut kernels off of cobs
In mixing bowl, gently stir together all ingredients
Serve and enjoy!

Corn Salsa

This one is another recipe that came about due to leftover corn from the previous shift. We were having Mexican food that day, and I didn't have the ingredients to make elotes, so using the ingredients I had on hand I came up with corn salsa. This recipe hasn't gone through any modifications from the beginning – every time I tried to make a change I felt it tasted better in it's original form. You don't have to zest the limes, I just do it to get more lime flavor without making the salsa too juicy. Whether you remove the ribs in the jalapenos depends on how spicy you like your salsa. If you like it spicy, by all means keep the ribs. If you are a mild salsa kind of person, remove the ribs (that's where the capsaicin, what gives peppers their heat resides) before dicing. You'll still get the slightly fruity flavor of the jalapenos without the heat. If you or someone you're sharing this with has the genetic variation affecting their olfactory receptor genes that ends up making cilantro taste like soap, simply replace it with parsley.

3 ears corn on the cob
2 jalapeno peppers, seeds removed then diced
$^1/_2$ large sweet onion, diced
$^1/_2$ bunch of cilantro, chopped
3 limes, zested then juiced
Pinch of salt to taste
Tortilla chips of choice

Cook, then chill corn on the cob (see Corn Caprese Salad recipe on page 60)
Cut kernels off cobs
Stir all ingredients together in a mixing bowl
Serve with tortilla chips

Guacamole

Everybody has their own idea of what guacamole should be. Everyone is entitled to their opinion, and since you're the one making it, use this recipe as a guideline and add or delete the things you want. I've always preferred my guac chunky, so after initially mashing it with a whisk I only fold the ingredients in. If you're a smooth guac kinda person, go ahead and mash away! Avocados are notorious for being difficult to have ripe at the perfect time. I usually buy underripe avocados a week before I will need them and let them ripen at room temperature in a paper bag. Once they're ripe, remove from the paper bag and store in the refrigerator for up to 3-4 days. To keep your guacamole from browning, you need to keep the avocado from browning. Leaving the pit on the guacamole doesn't work, but blanching the avocados will. Before cutting, bring a pot with enough water in it to cover the avocado to a boil. Gently lower one avocado into the water and leave for 10 seconds. Not 9, not 11. Remove using a slotted spoon and dunk into an ice bath. Repeat with your other avocados, making sure the water comes back up to a full boil each time before putting the next one in. I've found you seem to get deeper flavors from the aromatics if you crush them with some salt before adding them, so if you're traditional you can use a molcajete, but a muddler and a bowl or even a food processor will work.

1 small sweet onion, diced
2 jalapeno peppers, seeds removed (ribs removed if mild spice is desired)
2 cloves garlic
$1/2$ bunch cilantro, finely cut, divided
1 Tablespoon coarse ground salt
4 ripe Hass avocados, pitted with flesh removed
2 limes, zested and juiced, divided
Tortilla chips of choice

Make smooth paste of onion, jalapenos, garlic, half the cilantro, half the lime juice, and the salt
Using a whisk, mash the avocados and the paste in bowl
Add remaining cilantro, remaining lime juice, lime zest, and salt to taste
Fold to combine, serve immediately with tortilla chips

Hanky Panks

These have many names, but my Grandma Connie called them Hanky Panks, so I do also. Whatever you call them, very few people have not had these at a party sometime in their life. Simple to make, they work out perfect for assembling ahead of time and popping them in the oven just before serving.

1 pound ground chuck (80/20)
1 pound sweet Italian sausage
1 pound pasteurized prepared cheese product
1 Tablespoon ketchup
1 teaspoon worcestershire sauce
1 (1 pound) loaf cocktail rye bread

Brown ground chuck and Italian sausage, drain grease
Preheat oven to 350F
Melt pasteurized prepared cheese product in small saucepan or microwave
Stir tomato ketchup and Worcestershire sauce into melted cheese
Stir browned meat into mixture
Spoon approximately two Tablespoons of mixture on each slice of bread
Arrange in single layer on a baking sheet
Bake until lightly browned and crispy, about 10-15 minutes
Serve and enjoy!

Maple Roasted Brussels Sprouts with Bacon

First, the name. These tiny cabbage type vegetables were first cultivated in Belgium, home to Brussels. Therefore, they are referred to as Brussels sprouts, not brussel sprouts. I, like many, detested Brussels sprouts until I had one prepared properly. When boiled until mushy, they taste bitter and smell sulfurous. When roasted properly, they have a sweet, nutty flavor. When you add maple syrup you only amp up the sweetness, and what isn't made better by adding the umami salty punch of bacon?

1 pound Brussels sprouts, trimmed and halved
$^1/_4$ cup extra virgin olive oil
3 Tablespoons pure maple syrup (not the colored and flavored corn syrup)
4 slices bacon, cut into ½" pieces
$^1/_2$ teaspoon salt
$^1/_4$ teaspoon ground black pepper

Preheat oven to 400F
Place Brussels sprouts in mixing bowl and toss with olive oil and maple syrup
Spread Brussels sprouts in single layer on baking sheet
Sprinkle with bacon, salt, and pepper
Stirring halfway through, roast until bacon is crispy and sprouts are caramelized, about 45 minutes
Serve and enjoy!

Meatballs with Jelly Sauce

This is one of the easiest appetizers you can make. Premade meatballs, jelly, and chili sauce. The variations are endless, however. Grape jelly with chili sauce, orange marmalade with sweet chili sauce, orange marmalade with soy sauce, cranberry sauce, whatever combination you have a hankering for just give it a shot!

1 (32 ounce) bag frozen meatballs ($^1/_2$ ounce per meatball size)
1 $^1/_2$ cup chili sauce
10 ounces jelly

Mix all ingredients in slow cooker
Cover and cook for 2-3 hours on high or 4-6 hours on low
Serve and stand back!

Pimento Cheese

Sometimes called the caviar of the South, pimento cheese can be served on crackers or vegetables, in sandwiches, or scooped up with tortilla chips. Your mileage may vary, but I prefer a regular shred on the cheddar cheese as opposed to a fine shred. The flavor is the same, but I prefer the texture. Here is my recipe, if the one passed down through many generations in your family is different, keep making yours!

2 cups extra sharp cheddar cheese, shredded
8 ounces cream cheese, softened
$1/4$ cup mayonnaise
$1/4$ teaspoon garlic powder
$1/4$ teaspoon ground cayenne pepper
$1/4$ teaspoon onion powder
1 jalapeno pepper, seeded and diced (remove ribs if you don't want the heat)
1 (7 ounce) jar diced pimento, drained
Pinch of salt and ground black pepper to taste

Mix all ingredients on medium speed of stand mixer with paddle attachment
If you don't have a stand mixer, just combine all ingredients in a mixing bowl
Serve in manner of choice and enjoy!

Sausage Stuffed Cherry Pepper Poppers

These were brought in by another firefighter on one of our special days, and after one taste I had to get the recipe! These are great for bringing to a party, because you can make them up at home, throw them in the refrigerator, get dressed, and just pop them in the oven at the party. If you're making that many, a pound of sausage should make about 60 peppers.

$^1/_2$ pound sweet Italian sausage
2 (14 ounce) jars pickled red peppers
2 teaspoons olive oil
1 teaspoon chopped fresh parsley
Grated parmesan cheese

Preheat oven to 375F
Stuff about $^1/_2$ teaspoon of the sausage into each pepper
Toss peppers in a mixing bowl to coat with olive oil
Line rimmed baking sheet with nonstick foil
Bake until sausage is cooked through, about 20 minutes
Let cool slightly before serving
Sprinkle with parsley and Parmesan cheese
Serve and enjoy!

Shovel Dip

This is an adaptation of a simple diced tomatoes with green chilis and pasteurized prepared cheese product dip that a family friend makes. Why shovel dip? Just try not to shovel it in once you taste it!

1 pound Italian sausage
1 (10 ounce) can diced tomatoes with green chilis
8 ounces pasteurized prepared cheese product
$^1/_2$ teaspoon chili powder (recipe on page 160)

Brown the Italian sausage over medium high heat and drain the grease
Combine all ingredients in a slow cooker and cook on low 2-3 hours
Stir, turn slow cooker to warm, and serve with tortilla chips

Shrimp de Jonghe

If you're not from the northern Illinois area, you may have no idea what Shrimp de Jonghe is. Credit is given to the DeJonge brothers, who came to run a restaurant at the 1893 World's Columbian Exposition. It can be served in individual ramekins or out of a 7" x 11" casserole dish.

1 $^1/_2$ pounds shrimp, peeled and deveined
2 cups dry white wine
2 cups seasoned bread crumbs
1 cup melted butter
1 cup fresh parsley, chopped
2 cloves garlic, run through garlic press
$^1/_2$ teaspoon paprika
$^1/_4$ teaspoon cayenne pepper

Preheat oven to 350F
Lightly grease baking dish
Place shrimp evenly in dish
Pour wine over shrimp
Mix together bread crumbs, butter, parsley, garlic, paprika, and cayenne
Sprinkle bread crumb mixture over shrimp
Bake until shrimp are firm and topping is golden brown, about 20 minutes
Serve and enjoy!

Rescue Squads

Rescue squads were established to serve one of two purposes, depending on the department, either as extra manpower for whatever needed to be done on a fire scene or as a crew dedicated to rescuing firefighters that find themselves in a dangerous situation. Today, with the advent of Rapid Intervention Teams, departments mainly use Squad companies on fire scenes to help accomplish Ladder functions.

Heavy Rescue companies are more than just manpower wagons, though. Hazardous material incidents, vehicle and machinery extrication, dive rescues, building collapses, high angle rescues and more are the types of emergencies they may respond to. In addition to being the biggest toolbox the department has, squad companies are generally staffed with the most experienced firefighters due to the many varied demands placed on the company. Larger cities have dedicated crews assigned to the Squad, while many smaller cities may not have the call volume for a dedicated Squad company so an Engine company will be what's called a jump company. A jump company is assigned to both pieces of apparatus, but they only take the one dispatched for each particular incident. This means the vast majority of the time they respond on their Engine, but when necessary they respond on their Squad.

Some cities run the Squad company on two pieces of equipment. Some tow a trailer behind their squad vehicle, while others, like Chicago, have a heavy rescue type apparatus that runs with a snorkel apparatus. Once on scene they operate as a single company, but it is a good way to get the unique abilities of a snorkel without having to worry about the lack of equipment they can carry.

Still other cities rely on Medium Rescue apparatus, sometimes called Rescue Engines. These are a conventional Engine company that responds on a typical Engine that carries additional equipment for rescue purposes, such as extrication equipment, or hazardous materials equipment, or whatever their particular focus is.

Side Dishes

Whether it's the standard "meat and potatoes" or bread or a vegetable to go with your meal, often main dishes alone won't quite cut it. Complementary side dishes can not only elevate an entire meal, but can provide balance to the flavors in your main dish. Sides can range from asparagus to zucchini, from baked beans to yellow squash, from cabbage to... Okay, I don't have a side dish starting with "X", but you get the picture. There may be some old standards in your family that don't appear here, and there is one of two reasons for that. One, I don't have a recipe that I use for it, or two, I don't like whatever it is. That was one big advantage of being the cook – I didn't have to eat anything I didn't like. On the other side of the coin, how would that make you feel if the cook wouldn't eat something they made? It may be the best smelling, most delicious looking food ever but if the cook themself doesn't eat it, I'm wondering what's wrong with it!

Baked Potato Skins

Traditionally, when you order potato skins at your local watering hole, they are deep fried before being filled. While it's possible at home or the firehouse to fry using a deep pot, it's hard to do the volume you can by baking them. There's a couple reasons for the amount this recipe makes – it uses the amount of potato pulp needed to make enough baked potato soup for six firefighters (see recipe on page 103) and it makes enough potato skins for each person on a six person crew to have three skins. If you find you have more skins than you need for the meal you're making right now, just freeze the potato skins after baking them but before cooking them. When you're ready to make from frozen, just pull out how many you want from the freezer and let thaw on a plate on the countertop for an hour or so before making them. As I type this, and probably as you read this, I have a zipper bag full of empty, uncooked potato skins in my freezer waiting for the next time the mood strikes me! If your meal gets interrupted (happens all the time at the firehouse), reheat for 10 minutes at 350F. Using squeeze sour cream helps keep everything neat, and allowing everyone to top their own eases reheating if necessary. The first time I brought in the squeeze sour cream I took some jacking over the "space sour cream", but after everyone saw how easy it was for each person to get the amount they wanted without accidentally transferring what they were putting it on back into the container they were sold.

9 large baking potatoes, baked and cooled
$1/2$ cup vegetable oil
3 Tablespoons grated parmesan cheese
1 teaspoon season salt
$1/2$ teaspoon garlic powder
$1/2$ teaspoon onion powder
$1/2$ teaspoon paprika
$1/4$ teaspoon ground black pepper
4 cups cheddar cheese, shredded
1 $1/2$ pounds bacon, cooked and crumbled
Squeeze sour cream, 12 – 14 ounces, depending on size available at store
1 bunch green onions, sliced

Preheat oven to 475F

Cut potatoes in half lengthwise
Scoop out pulp, leaving about $1/4$ inch shell
Place potato shells open side up on greased baking sheet
Mix oil, salt, powders, paprika, and pepper
Brush oil mix over shells
Turn shells over, so open side is facing down
Brush oil mix over shells
Bake for 7 minutes
Pull baking sheet from oven, turn shells so they are open side up
Bake until edges start to brown and shells are crisp, about 7 more minutes
Pull from oven, fill shells with cheese and bacon
Return to oven, bake until cheese melts, about 2-3 minutes
Remove from oven, serve with sour cream and green onions

Basic Mashed Potatoes

There are other, more involved mashed potato recipes later in this section. Those are perfectly acceptable when you have the time, but sometimes you just don't. At the station, it may be a morning filled with runs, or a prescheduled multi-company drill – at home it may just be coming home from work too close to suppertime. From start to finish you could be eating mashed potatoes in about 30 minutes. Not peeling the potatoes helps timewise (the red skin is very thin) and so does not having to measure multiple ingredients. All of the rinsing helps to wash away the starch, which keeps your mashed potatoes fluffy instead of dense. If you have someone that isn't really into ranch dressing, don't worry. It's such a small amount compared to the potatoes you don't even taste a hint of ranch.

5 pound bag red skin potatoes
Ranch dressing

Clean the outside of the potatoes
Cut potatoes into 1 inch cubes, adding into cold water in pot when cut
When all potatoes are cut, dump into colander and rinse with cold water
When rinse water runs clear, put potatoes back into pot
Cover potatoes with hot water
Boil potatoes until soft, approximately 15 minutes
Dump potatoes into colander, rinse briefly with cold water
Put potatoes back into pot, add ½ cup ranch dressing
Mash with potato masher
Continue adding ranch dressing and mashing until potatoes are desired consistency

Beer Bread

To paraphrase Julia Child, I always cook with beer. Sometimes it even makes it into the food. There are very few beers my wife will take more than the smallest sip of, but this is her favorite bread recipe. Just make sure you don't use a bitter beer, because the bitterness seems to make it's way to the crust as the bread cooks. My preferred style of beer for drinking is IPA (you could say my blood type is IPA+) but I would absolutely recommend against using an IPA in this recipe. If desired, you could mix the dry ingredients ahead of time and store them for when needed, simply adding the beer and the butter.

2 $^1/_2$ cups self rising flour
$^1/_2$ cup all purpose flour
$^1/_4$ cup brown sugar
1 teaspoon baking powder
$^1/_2$ teaspoon salt
12 ounces beer, hefeweizen, bock, or Oktoberfest
$^1/_2$ stick lightly salted butter, melted

Preheat oven to 375F
Lightly grease a 9" x 5" loaf pan
Mix all dry ingredients in a bowl with the beer until just moistened
Transfer dough to bread pan
Top with the melted butter
Bake until top is browned and toothpick inserted in center comes out clean, 45-55 minutes
Cool on a wire rack
Slice, serve, and enjoy!

Best Ever Cornbread

There are those out there that profess not to care for cornbread. Personally, I think it may be due to trauma from their youth, trying to choke down a dry, crumbly mess. This is about the moistest, most flavorful cornbread I have run across, enough so that the first time someone made it at the station I absolutely had to have the recipe! If you like a little spice in your cornbread, you can use pepper jack cheese in place of the cheddar, or even mix some diced jalapenos in.

2 boxes (8 ounces each) corn muffin mix
$^2/_3$ cup milk
2 eggs
1 can (8 ounces) creamed corn
1 cup cheddar cheese, shredded (or pepper jack cheese, shredded)
Diced jalapeno peppers, optional
Lightly salted butter, softened, for topping if desired
Drizzle of honey, for topping if desired

Preheat oven to 400F
Mix cornbread as directed on package
Stir in creamed corn and cheese (and jalapenos if using)
Pour into lightly greased 9" x 13" dish
Bake until top is golden brown and toothpick inserted in center comes out clean, 20-25 minutes
Slice, serve, and enjoy!

BLT Pasta Salad

Bacon, Lettuce, and Tomato sandwiches have always been a staple of summertime dining in my family, taking advantage of the bountiful nature of tomato plants in home gardens. While fresh tomatoes are available in pretty much every supermarket year round across the USA, the tomatoes available in the winter never seemed to measure up to the summer tomatoes. Not wanting to limit our BLT eating to a few short months, we came up with this pasta salad after some hits and definite misses. Just keep in mind as you're preparing this, you want the pasta a little firmer than if you were eating it hot.

1 box (16 ounces) medium shell pasta (or preferred pasta)
1 $^1/_4$ pounds cherry tomatoes, quartered
$^2/_3$ cup mayonnaise
$^1/_2$ cup cheddar cheese, finely shredded
5 stalks celery, diced
5 green onions, thin sliced
$^1/_4$ teaspoon salt (or to taste)
$^1/_8$ teaspoon ground black pepper (or to taste)
1 pound package bacon, sliced into approximately 1 inch squares

Put pasta in a pot, cover with salted water
Bring to a boil
Stir, turn off the heat, and cover
After 8 minutes, check if the pasta is done to your liking
Drain and rinse with cold water until chilled
Pour pasta into large bowl
Stir in tomatoes, mayonnaise, cheese, celery, green onions, salt, and pepper until combined
Cover and chill for at least two hours
Just before serving, cook bacon over med-high heat, stirring occasionally
When bacon is crispy, about ten minutes, remove from pan and drain on paper towels
Mix bacon into other ingredients and serve

Cilantro Lime Rice

As evidenced by many fast food burrito places out there, cilantro lime rice goes very well with Mexican food. As in other recipes involving cilantro, if needed it can be replaced with parsley.

2 cups water
1 cup long grain white rice
1 chicken bouillon cube
2 Tablespoons fresh lime juice
2 Tablespoons fresh cilantro (or parsley), chopped
Pinch of salt to taste

Over high heat, bring water, rice, and bouillon to a boil
When mixture boils, reduce heat to med-low, and cover with a tight fitting lid
Simmer until rice is tender, 20-25 minutes
Remove from heat, stir in lime juice, cilantro/parsley, and salt
Fluff with a fork
Serve and enjoy!

Cole Slaw

There are many styles of cole slaw out there – this one goes well with barbecue, especially pulled pork or smoked brisket. It's use is not limited to those dishes, however. Any time you want a side dish that's crunchy, creamy, a little tart, and a little sweet this fits the bill. If desired, instead of sugar, you can use the equivalent amount of sugar substitute. If substituting, make sure to use a sugar substitute that the flavor isn't too prominent and only provides sweetness. If you prefer not to use bagged cole slaw mix, shred approximately 12 ounces of green cabbage and mix with two ounces of matchstick cut carrots.

1 bag (14 ounces) cole slaw mix
2 Tablespoons sweet onion, very finely diced
$^1/_2$ cup mayonnaise
$^1/_2$ cup white sugar (or sugar substitute equivalent)
1 Tablespoon white vinegar
$^1/_2$ teaspoon poppy seeds
$^1/_4$ teaspoon salt

Mix the cole slaw mix and onions in a large bowl
In a separate bowl, whisk together the mayonnaise, sugar, vinegar, poppy seeds, and salt, making the dressing mixture
Pour dressing mixture over the cole slaw mix
Stir to coat all of the cole slaw mix
Cover and chill for at least two hours
Just before serving, give mix one last stir, then serve and enjoy!

Corn Casserole

Apparently I led a sheltered life. I had never had this recipe until I was working part time at the local blood bank and we had a mobile blood drive in a small town at the VFW. The Ladies Auxiliary had a potluck for those who donated and those of us working. After one bite, I had them track down who had made it and got the recipe from her. After that, I made it numerous times at the station, plus it's a must on holidays now.

2 sticks salted butter, divided
2 cans (15 ounce) whole kernel sweet corn, drained
2 cans (14.75 ounce) creamed corn
2 boxes (8.5 ounce) corn muffin mix
16 ounces sour cream
4 eggs, beaten

Preheat oven to 350F
Mix one stick melted butter, corn, creamed corn, muffin mix, sour cream, and eggs in a mixing bowl
Melt one stick of butter in the bottom of a 9" x 13" casserole dish
Remove dish from oven when butter is melted
Ensure entire bottom of dish is covered in butter
Pour mix from bowl into dish
Bake until top is golden brown, about 50-55 minutes
Serve and enjoy!

Creamed Corn

Creamed anything is usually thought of as what you make when you can't afford anything else. Anyone who has ever eaten at Lawry's Prime Rib in Beverly Hills, Chicago, Dallas, or Las Vegas, can verify that done their way, creamed corn is anything but. At one time, they had their recipe right on their website, so I shamelessly stole…er, copied it and usually made it up for special occasions at the firehouse.

3 Tablespoons salted butter
3 Tablespoons all purpose flour
1 teaspoon salt
3 cups heavy whipping cream
2 pounds frozen sweet corn
4 Tablespoons white sugar

Melt butter in a heavy saucepan
Add flour and salt, stirring to blend
Slowly add whipping cream, stirring constantly until thickened
Add corn and sugar, heat until corn is hot (make sure it doesn't boil)
Serve and stand back!

Easiest Corn on the Cob

I've seen hundreds of ways to cook corn on the cob, all the way from smoking it, to in an empty dishwasher, to soaking it with the husk on and grilling it I'm not going to list them all because I've probably already lost some of you by now. The easiest, most foolproof way I have found is the way I already shared in the corn caprese salad recipe on page 60.

6 ears corn on the cob, shucked
2 Tablespoons white sugar (optional)
Juice of one lemon or lime (optional)

In a large pot, bring enough water to a boil to cover all the cobs
Mix in the sugar and juice if using
Put cobs in boiling water
Shut off heat, cover, and let sit for 10 minutes
Remove cobs from water, serve and enjoy!

Easy Cheesy Potatoes

A local store here in town (one of the only neighborhood grocery stores left) makes frozen cheesy potatoes that are incredible with almost any meal. The previous generation owner, even though he was a big fan of the Fire Department, would never give me the recipe. Smart move, since even though it is on the other side of town, I drive over there on a pretty regular basis. Every time I go, even if it's not planned for the meal I'm going there for, I pick up a tray of the cheesy potatoes to keep in the freezer for when we want them. There are only a few stations close enough to the store to be able to go there on duty, so when I wasn't at one of those stations, I came up with this version of it that I feel is 98% as good as his. Every time I tried something different after I settled on the recipe below, I felt it slipped further away from being so close, so this is what I stuck with.

1 bag (30 ounces) country style shredded hash brown potatoes
16 ounces sour cream
2 cups cheddar cheese, shredded
1 can (10.75 ounces) cream of chicken soup
1 cup sweet onion, diced
1 stick salted butter, melted
1 Tablespoon garlic powder

Preheat oven to 350F
Combine all ingredients in mixing bowl
Pour into ungreased 9" x 13" casserole dish
Bake until golden brown on top, 50-55 minutes

French Onion and Bacon Mashed Potatoes

These are almost as easy as the Basic Mashed Potatoes on page 74, but with these you get a ton of flavor out of the items you add in. If you're pressed for time, you can use the premade bacon found by the salad stuff in the grocery store. Make sure it's real bacon and not the fake crumbles. The amount of dip you need depends on the potatoes you use. With Yukon Golds you end up needing the entire package of French onion dip, but that same amount with redskin potatoes would make you think this is a recipe for soup.

5 pounds potatoes, peeled if necessary
1 pound bacon, diced (or prepackaged crumbled real bacon, 4+ ounces)
1 package (16 ounces) french onion dip

Cut potatoes into 1 inch cubes, adding into cold water in pot when cut
When all potatoes are cut, dump into colander and rinse with cold water
When rinse water runs clear, put potatoes back into pot
Cover potatoes with hot water
Boil potatoes until soft, approximately 15 minutes
If using uncooked bacon, cook in med-high skillet until crisp, about 10 minutes
Remove bacon from skillet and drain on paper towels
Dump potatoes into colander, rinse briefly with cold water
Put back into boiling pot
Add in half of dip, mash, keep adding dip until desired consistency
Add in bacon
Serve and enjoy!

Fried Cabbage

When I was newer on the job, I worked with a cook that liked to shake things up every now and then when it came to side dishes. This was his favorite to make with hearty dishes, or when he got tired of potatoes. Bacon, onion, garlic, what's not to like? I liked it so much, when I became full time cook, I didn't wait until I was tired of potatoes to make it – I made potatoes when I was tired of cabbage! Leftovers taste just as good as the original meal when microwaved, or you can use it as a base for any recipe that has cooked cabbage in it.

$1/2$ pound bacon, chopped
1 large sweet onion, rough chop
2 cloves garlic, run through garlic press
1 large head green cabbage, cored and rough chop
1 Tablespoon season salt
1 teaspoon ground black pepper
$1/2$ teaspoon garlic powder
$1/2$ teaspoon onion powder
$1/4$ teaspoon paprika

Cook bacon in large stock pot over med-high heat until crispy, about 10 minutes
Add onion, cook until caramelized, stirring constantly, about 10 minutes
Add garlic, stir a few times to mix into the bacon and onion
Add cabbage, cook for 10 minutes, stirring occasionally
Add rest of ingredients, reduce heat to low and cover
Cook for 30 minutes, stirring occasionally
Serve and enjoy!

Garlic Bread

They say man does not live by bread alone, but man does not live by a meal without bread, either. What follows is what my Italian friend and former Lieutenant calls "Dago Bait". The perfect accompaniment to your pasta and sugo you just made!

1 pound loaf Italian bread, the softer and denser the better
1 stick salted butter, softened
1 clove garlic, run through garlic press
Grated parmesan cheese
Oregano

Preheat oven to 375F
Slice the bread into 1" or so slices, I usually ended up with 12
Mix the garlic into the butter using a fork
Using the back side of a spoon, spread the butter evenly on the bread
Sprinkle parmesan on the bread, covering the bread
Sprinkle oregano over the parmesan

Cook 10-15 minutes
Remove from cooking tray and place on paper towels on table – you may want to use a spatula to take the bread off the tray since it's rather warm at this point, having just come out of the oven. I knew the guys that never quite figured out the spatula trick and always asked them to help get the bread off the tray to watch them as they burned their fingers. Of course while they were taking a minute to cool their fingers, I was stuck holding the heavy, hot cookie sheet, so who's the laugh on?

Garlic Rosemary Red Potatoes

Sometimes you're making something Italian-esque, and need some potatoes to go with it. In addition to being rather tasty, these are super easy to make. These can get a little sticky when it comes to the baking sheet, so if you're not using non-stick foil or parchment paper, make sure to spray some non-stick cooking spray before cooking. If you're looking for an easy way to cover a baking sheet during cooking that's also easy to remove, just use another baking sheet of the same size upside down over the one you're cooking on.

4 pounds red skin potatoes, washed and cubed to about ¾" cubes
1 stick butter, melted
3 cloves garlic, run through garlic press
Juice of 2 lemons
2 teaspoons season salt
1 ½ teaspoons rosemary
2 Tablespoons grated parmesan cheese

Preheat oven to 350F
Mix potatoes, butter, garlic, lemon juice, season salt, and rosemary in large mixing bowl until potatoes are evenly coated
Pour onto baking sheet in a single layer
Sprinkle parmesan cheese over potatoes
Bake, covered, for 30 minutes
Uncover, continue baking until golden brown and tender, about another 10 minutes
Serve and enjoy!

Green Beans with Bacon and Garlic

I'm not really someone who "has to have" vegetables (I see you smirking, Al and Bill), but these are right up my alley. One pan, 20 minutes, bacon and garlic, what's not to love? You can just trim the ends off of the beans if you like, or you can cut or rip them down to a couple inches long for easy stirring and eating. If it's the middle of winter, you can even use frozen green beans – they don't need to be fully thawed, just what they get from rinsing them. Don't worry about getting all the moisture off of the green beans, the residual moisture helps to steam them while they sauté. Make sure you just leave enough bacon grease to have a thin layer on the bottom of the pan, if there's any more the beans will be greasy. You can use preground black pepper if you want, but this is one that benefits from fresh ground black pepper.

1 pound bacon, diced
2 pounds green beans, trimmed
6 cloves garlic, run through garlic press
2 teaspoons ground black pepper

Heat skillet or cast iron pan over med-high heat
Add bacon, cook until crisp, about 6 or 7 minutes
Rinse green beans in a colander
Remove all but a thin layer of bacon grease from pan
Add green beans to pan, stir to coat with the bacon grease
Cover, stirring occasionally, until they start to char but still have some bite, about 6 minutes (if you prefer firmer green beans, 4 minutes)
Add garlic, stir constantly for 1 minute
Remove from heat, add pepper, stir to mix thoroughly
Serve and enjoy!

Loaded Mashed Potatoes

A fully loaded baked potato can be the perfect foil to a rich meal. This is a mashed potato version of that. The creaminess of mashed vs. baked potatoes help put this dish over the top.

5 pounds russet potatoes, peeled and cubed into 1" chunks
1 pound bacon, diced
8 ounces cream cheese, room temperature
1 cup sour cream
1 stick salted butter, melted
2 $1/2$ cups cheddar cheese, shredded, divided
5 green onions, sliced thin
2 teaspoons salt
$1/2$ teaspoon ground black pepper

Boil potatoes until tender, about 30 minutes
While potatoes are boiling, cook bacon in large skillet until crisp, about 10 minutes
Remove bacon from skillet and drain on paper towels
Preheat oven to 350F
When potatoes are tender, rinse with cold water in colander and return to pot
Add cream cheese, sour cream, and butter to potatoes, mash until smooth
Add 2 cups of the cheddar cheese, green onions, half the bacon, salt, and pepper
Stir until well combined
Transfer to buttered 9" x 13" casserole dish
Top with remaining cheese
Bake until top is golden, about 30 minutes
Top with remaining bacon
Serve and enjoy!

Oriental Salad

I got this recipe from my friend who was my officer for a couple years, then later became Chief of the department. Crunchy, tangy, sweet, this salad is a great accompaniment to almost any meal, or can be turned into a light summer supper by adding grilled chicken strips. You can make this ahead of time, just wait until serving to pour the dressing on the salad.

Salad
3 heads romaine lettuce
1 head cauliflower
2 bunches green onions
1 pound chopped pecans
3 packages oriental flavor ramen noodles
$1/2$ stick butter

Dressing
1 cup vegetable oil
1 cup brown sugar
$1/2$ cup white vinegar
$1/2$ cup soy sauce
Flavor packets from Ramen noodles

Chop and mix lettuce, cauliflower, green onions, and pecans
Break up noodles from Ramen into small chunks
Constantly stirring, fry noodles in butter until they start to toast, about 5 minutes
Add noodles to salad mix
Mix all dressing ingredients, shake well
Drizzle dressing over salad, toss well
Serve immediately and try not to get run over!

Oven Roasted Veggies

There are myriad ways to prepare veggies, but for large chunk type vegetables like broccoli or cauliflower I like this simple method using frozen veggies. As with other recipes made on a baking sheet, use non-stick foil or parchment paper, or use non-stick cooking spray on the baking sheet to prevent sticking.

2 pounds frozen broccoli florets or cauliflower
1 Tablespoon olive oil
1 $^1/_2$ teaspoons Montreal steak seasoning (use prepared or see recipe on page 162)

Preheat oven to 400F
Spread veggies out in single layer
Drizzle olive oil over veggies
Sprinkle steak seasoning over veggies
Cook until veggies are heated through but not mushy, about 20 minutes
Serve and enjoy!

Parmesan Mashed Potatoes

Several years ago, while on a trip to leave as much of our money as possible with the giant mouse in Florida, we went to the prime rib buffet at one of the hotels. The prime rib was great, as prime rib always is unless you overcook it. What stole the show was the mashed potatoes. I asked one of the chefs for the recipe, and he actually gave it to me! Years later I saw it posted on the interwebz, so I'm not giving out any top secrets here. Well, at least I'm not the first one giving out the secret!

3 pounds potatoes, peeled and cubed into 1" cubes
2 cups half & half
$^1/_2$ stick salted butter
1 cup grated parmesan cheese
1 Tablespoon salt
1 teaspoon ground white pepper

Boil the potatoes until tender, about 30 minutes
Rinse potatoes with cold water in colander
Return potatoes to pot they were boiled in
Heat half & half in small sauce pan and add to potatoes
Mash potatoes with potato masher
When potatoes are smooth, add in butter and parmesan
Stir in salt and white pepper
Serve and dream of Florida!

Pickle Potatoes

There are no pickles anywhere in these potatoes, but the first time I made them for my kids, I used the wavy slicer so the potato slices looked like pickles. The name stuck. This is pretty much the only time I don't peel the potatoes when using Yukon Golds. You want to slice the onions as thin as you can, so they pretty much disappear into the dish, only contributing flavor.

5 pounds Yukon Gold potatoes, washed and sliced into about ¼" slices
$^1/_4$ sweet onion, sliced very thin
2 Tablespoons season salt, divided
1 stick salted butter, sliced into pats

Preheat oven to 375F
Spray covered dish or roasting pan with non-stick cooking spray
Put half the potatoes in dish/pan
Spread onion slices on top of potatoes
Sprinkle half of season salt on top of potatoes
Put rest of potatoes in dish/pan
Arrange butter pats evenly over top of potatoes
Cover and cook in oven for 30 minutes
Remove from oven, stir, replace back in oven
Cook for another 30 minutes, until potatoes are tender
Stir one last time, serve, and enjoy!

Potato Cakes

When you end up with leftover mashed potatoes from one meal, these are a way to reuse them in a new dish. While these are different from traditional potato pancakes (latkes), you can top them with the traditional toppings, such as sour cream or applesauce. You can also add a little cheese surprise in the middle by placing some shredded cheese on the top of the potatoes while they are frying and covering with more potatoes, then flipping and finishing cooking.

4 cups mashed potatoes
2 eggs, beaten
1 cup all purpose flour
1 teaspoon salt
2 Tablespoons salted butter
Squeeze sour cream, 12 – 14 ounces, depending on size available at store
16 ounces applesauce for topping, optional

In mixing bowl, combine potatoes, eggs, flour, and salt, mix well
Melt butter in large frying pan or on griddle over low heat
Drop 4" circles of potato mix into pan or onto griddle
Pat to flatten to about ½" thick
Cook until bottom is browned, about 10 minutes
Flip and cook until other side is browned, about 10 minutes
Serve and enjoy!

Strawberry Spinach Salad

I'm not much of a salad guy, and neither is my Dad. This is the salad my Mom makes that we both will eat, so almost any time we get together with my parents, this is what we ask her to make. She got the recipe from my Aunt, and the only change I made is to add the gorgonzola, because I like the contrast between the dryness of the cheese and the sweetness of the strawberries. If your family (or crew) are like my good friend and former Lieutenant and aren't particularly keen on gorgonzola, serve it on the side. I made the mistake of mixing it all together and pissed him off something fierce since the salad was all he was planning on eating that day…

Dressing
1 cup olive oil
$^1/_2$ cup white sugar
$^1/_3$ cup white wine vinegar
1 $^1/_2$ Tablespoons minced onions
1 $^1/_2$ Tablespoons poppy seeds
1 teaspoon dry mustard powder
1 teaspoon salt

Salad
2 cups pecan or walnut halves
6 Tablespoons melted butter
4 cups sliced strawberries
2 bags (8 ounces each) spinach
1 container (5 ounces) gorgonzola crumbles

Combine all dressing ingredients in covered container, shake well
Refrigerate dressing overnight
Preheat oven to 350F
Mix nuts and butter, toast on rimmed baking sheet for 10 minutes
Combine nuts, strawberries, spinach, cheese, and dressing
Toss to coat, serve and enjoy!

Yeast Rolls

Light, airy, a little sweet, these are great to eat and almost as easy to make! The dough does end up rather sticky, resist the temptation to add more flour and make the rolls too heavy.

2 cups hot water
$^1/_4$ cup and 2 Tablespoons white sugar
$^1/_4$ cup vegetable shortening
2 packages (0.25 ounce) active dry yeast
4 $^1/_2$ cups all purpose flour
2 eggs, beaten
2 teaspoons salt

In a large bowl, mix the hot water, white sugar, and shortening
Allow to cool until lukewarm
Mix in yeast until dissolved
Mix in the flour, eggs, and salt
Allow to rise until doubled in size
Grease 16 muffin cups
Divide the dough into the muffin cups and allow to rise until doubled in size
Preheat oven to 425F
Bake for 10 minutes, or until a toothpick comes out clean
Serve and enjoy!

Fire Vocabulary, Part 2

In this section of Fire vocabulary, I'll use the more traditional term then definition style, since most of these definitions generally only have one name.

Backdraft – When a fire has consumed all of the oxygen in a closed space, yet continues to smolder. When air is reintroduced improperly, the fire roars back to life, resembling an explosion

Bugles – Used to signify an officer's rank on their collar. In honor of the speaking trumpets Chiefs used to relay orders in the early days of the US fire service

Cavitation – When air is allowed into the pump on a pumping apparatus. This causes the pump to be very inefficient and unreliable

Cockloft – A void space above a ceiling and below the structural supports of the roof. Fire can spread rapidly and undetected within a large building through the cockloft

Conduction – The transfer of heat through a medium, such as when metal pipe is heated by fire on one side of a wall, the pipe conducts the heat to the other side of the wall

Convection – Transfer of heat or fire by the fact that heat rises

Defensive attack – Generally an exterior fire attack, when the fire building is too unsafe to fight the fire inside, also referred to as "surround and drown"

Exposure – Another combustible adjacent to something that is on fire that is in danger of having (or has had) fire transfer to it from the original fire, by conduction, convection, direct flame impingement, or radiation

Extrication – Removal of a trapped victim through the use of tools, whether hand tools or powered tools, such as air, electric, or hydraulic

FDC (Fire Department Connection) – Where a pumping apparatus connects to a building's sprinkler and/or standpipe system

Fire tetrahedron – The four things necessary for combustion – fuel, oxygen, heat, and/or a continuous chemical reaction

Flashover – When all combustibles in a closed space all reach their ignition temperature, results in the entire room being on fire, including the air

Forcible entry – Using force to gain entry to a building or area by disabling or bypassing security devices. Can be as simple as kicking in a door, or using hand or power tools

Forward lay – When a water supply hoseline is advanced from a hydrant towards the fire scene

Friction loss – Reduction of flow within a hose caused by friction between the water and the inside of the hose. Friction loss is determined by the diameter and type of hose, the length of hose the water is traveling through, and the amount of water flowing. The Engineer uses friction loss to determine the pressure to have the pump deliver through a hoseline

Horizontal ventilation – Using either existing wind or providing airflow with a mechanical fan to exhaust hot smoke and gases

Interior attack – When the fire is fought from inside the building. Interior attack minimizes damage to the structure by limiting the spread of the fire, which reduces the smoke generated, and also by reducing the water used for extinguishment

Master stream – A device, either portable or mounted, with a large nozzle capable of flowing 350 gallons per minute or more of water

Mutual aid – an agreement between departments to assist each other when additional manpower or equipment are required, generally requested when multiple alarms are asked for by the Incident Commander

Mutual response – Similar to mutual aid, but on initial dispatch, so either the closest appropriate apparatus responds regardless of department or equipment one department is lacking is automatically provided by another department

Overhaul – After the fire is extinguished, overhaul is performed to ensure there is no hidden fire still burning, done to prevent a rekindle. Overhaul involves removing wall coverings, ceiling, etc…

Radiation – Heat transfer by means of infrared energy

Rekindle – When overhaul misses a hidden fire still burning. Usually, the rekindle causes more damage than the initial fire

Residual pressure – The amount of pressure in a water system when a hydrant is fully open

Reverse lay – When the water supply hoseline is advanced from the fire scene towards the hydrant

Solid stream – Stream of water from a round orifice nozzle. Called such since the stream is solid water, as opposed to a straight stream

Static pressure – The pressure in a water system when water is not flowing

Straight stream – Steam of water from an adjustable nozzle, where water passes a round baffle through a round orifice, resulting in a hollow stream of water

Vertical ventilation - Using holes created in the roof to exhaust hot smoke and gases thanks to convection

Water hammer – Large, damaging shock wave caused by shutting a valve or nozzle too quickly

Soups, Stews, and Chilis

Here in Northern Illinois, not only do we have all four seasons, but sometimes all in the same day! We have a saying that if you don't like the weather, wait 10 minutes and it'll change. When the weather starts trending colder nothing makes for a better supper than a steaming bowl of goodness in front of you. These recipes are not limited to supper, however. For lunch to warm up the kids after playing outside in the snow, as a side with a meal, it's hard to think of a time that would be bad for a good soup, stew, or chili. For the dishes with noodles, you can use whatever noodle you like to create a new dish from the same recipe.

Broth

A broth or a stock is the base of any soup or stew, so what better place to start this chapter? First, what's the difference between broth and stock? Both are prepared similarly, but there are some key differences. Both are simmered with mirepoix (a fancy way of saying carrots, celery, and onion) and aromatic herbs. Broth is any liquid that has had meat cooked in it. Broth can have bones as part of the mix, but it doesn't have to. Broths are typically seasoned, so it can be sipped on its own. Stock is made by simmering bones (which can have meat on them) and is left unseasoned. Poultry broth is easy to make, cheap, and can be used in almost anything. I use poultry broth in place of beef broth – even my beef barley vegetable soup doesn't end up tasting chicken-y.

The minimum ratio you want to have is one pound of poultry per quart of water. Any more poultry and you'll just have a richer broth, which definitely isn't a bad thing. You end up with slightly different flavors depending on which parts of the chicken you use. Traditionally, before there were entire restaurant chains devoted to chicken wings, wings were used for broth. Now that wings have gone from a dirt cheap extra piece that people didn't want to being in demand, I prefer to use leg quarters. They provide plenty of flavor, plenty of gelatin for body, and they usually cost less than five bucks for 10 pounds. For turkey broth, Thanksgiving makes things easy – what else are you going to do with the carcass and the neck? If you have a vegetarian in your life, you can use this same recipe to make vegetable broth. Just leave out the poultry, and either adjust the amount of veggies up to the amount of water, or just use less water. To get a little more of that umami going, you might want to add in some mushrooms regardless of which broth you're making, but especially if you're making vegetable broth.

I put measured half gallons of the broth in gallon freezer zip bags, get all the air out before sealing, and freeze flat to take up less room in the freezer. That works out well for most of my recipes, since most of them call for a half gallon of broth. To thaw you can either take a bag out of the freezer and put it in the refrigerator a day or two before you'll need it, or put in a sink full of cold water for an hour or two. Once the weather turned cool, I tried to always have broth in the freezer, which meant I made broth once a month or so.

Broth, continued

10 pounds chicken leg quarters or a turkey carcass & neck
5 carrots, sliced
5 celery ribs, sliced
5 cloves garlic, crushed
5 sprigs parsley
3 bay leaves
3 sweet onions, rough chop
10 quarts water
$\frac{1}{4}$ cup salt (or to taste)
Ground black pepper to taste

Combine all ingredients except salt and pepper in a large stock pot
Bring to a simmer over low heat
Maintain just enough of a simmer that steam rises from the surface
Simmer for an hour and a half
Season with salt and pepper to taste
Strain through a fine mesh strainer, then let cool
Pick meat (if using) off of bones and save for future use
Transfer to containers and refrigerate until chilled, about six hours
Skim any fat or scum off of surface
Use within 5 days if refrigerated or six months if freezing

Baked Potato Soup

This one goes great on a day that you make baked potato skins (see recipe on page 72) for another meal. If you're making the potato skins and will be making the soup on another day, just freeze the flesh for when you need it. Make sure to label it, however – I was planning on making baked potato soup using flesh I had in the freezer, but when I thawed it I discovered it was pizza dough I had frozen for later use! I found out later that someone on another shift had their own surprise – they wanted to make pizza with my leftover dough and thawed my potato flesh. The local pizza place was very appreciative, though, since both shifts ended up ordering from them because we didn't have the other ingredients we needed to use what we thawed.

$^1/_2$ pound bacon, diced
$^2/_3$ cup butter
$^2/_3$ cup all purpose flour
6 cups whole milk
Pulp from 9 baking potatoes
10 ounces cheddar cheese, shredded, divided
1 bunch green onions, chopped, divided
$^1/_2$ Tablespoon salt
1 teaspoon ground black pepper
1 container (8 ounce) sour cream

In a skillet over medium heat, cook bacon until crispy, about 10 minutes
Drain bacon on paper towels, reserve
In large pot over medium heat, melt butter
Stir in flour and cook for about 1 minute
Whisk in milk, a little at a time, stirring constantly until thickened
Stir in potatoes, 2/3 of the bacon, 2/3 of the cheese, 2/3 of the green onions, and the salt and pepper
Cook until thoroughly heated
Stir in sour cream, heat for 2-3 more minutes
Serve with the remaining bacon, cheese, and green onions for topping

Beef Barley Vegetable Soup

Savory is the best word I can come up with to describe this soup. Every time I take a bite, I reflexively do that eyes closed "Ummm." If you want to make things easier on yourself, you can use two 12 ounce packages of frozen mixed vegetables instead of the separate bags of veggies. Just beware that frozen mixed veggies have carrots, which are already in the soup, and most also include lima beans. If those two things aren't a dealbreaker for you, go ahead and use the frozen mixed veggies. A good accompaniment to this soup would be a hearty bread, a delicate yeast roll might get steamrolled by everything going on within the soup. This recipe can also be made in a pressure cooker if you have one and the day's schedule doesn't cooperate with doing the stovetop version.

1 (3 pound) chuck roast
1 Tablespoon vegetable oil
3 carrots, sliced
3 ribs celery, sliced
1 sweet onion, rough chop
1 clove garlic, run through garlic press
1 quart homemade chicken broth
1 box (750 grams, 26.46 ounces) Pomi® chopped tomatoes
$1/2$ cup barley
1 Tablespoon white sugar
$1/4$ teaspoon ground black pepper
2 bay leaves
8 ounces frozen sweet corn
8 ounces frozen peas
8 ounces frozen green beans
1 Tablespoon salt (or to taste)
1 teaspoon ground black pepper (or to taste)

Cut beef into bite size pieces
Heat 1 Tablespoon vegetable oil in stock pot over med-high heat
Add beef, cook until browned on all sides, stirring frequently
Remove meat and set aside
Reduce heat to medium, stir in carrots
Sauté carrots for 5 minutes, stirring frequently

Stir in celery, sauté with carrots for 5 minutes, stirring frequently

Stir in onion, sauté with carrots and celery until soft, about 5 minutes, stirring frequently

Add garlic, saute for 1 minute, stirring constantly

Add broth, tomatoes, barley, sugar, pepper, and bay leaves; bring to a simmer

Simmer, covered, until beef is tender and barley is cooked

Add frozen vegetables in the last half hour of cooking time

Serve and enjoy!

Pressure Cooker Beef Barley Vegetable Soup

Use the same ingredients as above

Set pressure cooker to Sauté

When the pot is hot, add the vegetable oil and beef

Stirring frequently, sauté beef until brown on all sides

Add carrots, celery, and onion

Stir and scrape up any bits off the bottom, cook until soft, about 10 minutes

Add garlic, stir and cook for one minute

Add broth, tomatoes, barley, sugar, pepper, and bay leaves; stir to mix

Put lid on pot, set steam release knob to sealing position

Cancel Sauté mode, pressure cook for 20 minutes (the pot will be pretty full, so it will take several minutes to come to pressure)

When cooking cycle ends, let pot naturally release pressure for 15 minutes

While waiting for pot to release pressure, cook frozen veggies according to directions on bag

When pot is done releasing pressure, stir in cooked frozen veggies

Serve and enjoy!

Buffalo Chicken Chili

Chili with the flavors of Buffalo wings? Why not? Serve with the traditional wing accoutrements, or traditional chili toppings, or if you're feeding a big crew, why not both? Celery chunks, carrot chunks, bleu cheese or ranch dressing, shredded cheese, sour cream, crushed corn chips, let your imagination run wild for the toppings you put out!

1 Tablespoon vegetable oil
2 Tablespoons lightly salted butter
2 pound boneless skinless chicken breast, cubed
1 large sweet onion, rough chop
$1/4$ cup chili powder (see recipe on page 160)
2 Tablespoons ground cumin
1 Tablespoon paprika
1 teaspoon salt
$1/2$ teaspoon ground black pepper
4 cloves garlic, run through garlic press
1 can (29 ounces) tomato sauce
1 can (19 ounces) red kidney beans
1 can (15 ounces) white kidney beans (cannellini)
1 can (15 ounces) crushed tomatoes
$1/2$ cup hot Buffalo wing sauce

Heat oil and butter in large pot over med-high heat
Add chicken to pot, cook and stir until chicken is done, about 7-10 minutes
Stir in onion, chili powder, cumin, paprika, salt, and pepper
Cook and stir until the onion is soft, about 5 minutes
Add garlic, cook for 1 minute while stirring constantly
Stir in tomato sauce, beans, crushed tomatoes, and wing sauce
Bring to a boil, reduce heat to simmer
Simmer for at least one hour
Serve with toppings of choice

Chicken and Dumpling Stew

Who doesn't like chicken and dumplings? My bet is only people who have never had it! This version of it has the added bonus of being super easy but still as savory as Mom's that she made when you were young.

Half gallon chicken broth
6 boneless skinless chicken breasts, cubed
2 large sweet onions, rough chop
1 pound baby carrots
5 celery ribs, sliced
2 bay leaves
1 teaspoon salt
$1/2$ teaspoon ground black pepper
4 $1/2$ cups baking mix
1 $1/3$ cups milk

Combine chicken broth, chicken, onion, carrots, celery, bay leaves, salt and pepper in large pot
Bring to a boil, cover pot, and reduce to simmer
Simmer until chicken is done and veggies are tender, about 20-25 minutes
Mix baking mix and milk until dough is sticky
Drop golf ball sized pieces of dough into stew
Cover pot and cook until dumplings are cooked through, about 10 minutes
Serve and enjoy!

Better than Penicillin Chicken Noodle Soup

What mother didn't serve their kids some chicken noodle soup when they were feeling under the weather? Scientific studies have actually found that chicken soup can help fight a cold. It helps clear congestion, as well as thins mucus, and has a mild anti-inflammatory effect that can help ease symptoms. You can use whatever noodle you prefer, but you really owe it to yourself to try Reames® noodles, found in the frozen food section. If you have chicken left over from making your broth, you can use that in place of the chicken breasts.

3 boneless skinless chicken breasts, cooked and diced
2 Tablespoons salted butter
4 carrots, sliced
5 ribs celery, sliced
1 large sweet onion, rough chop
2 cloves garlic, run through garlic press
1 half gallon of prepared chicken broth
2 bay leaves
8 ounces frozen sweet corn
8 ounces frozen peas
8 ounces frozen green beans
1 package (16 ounce) Reames® noodles
1 Tablespoon salt (or to taste)
1 teaspoon ground black pepper to taste

Melt butter in large pot over medium heat
Add in carrot slices, stirring occasionally, cook for 5 minutes
Add in celery slices, stirring occasionally, cook for 5 minutes
Add in onion, stirring occasionally, cook until just about soft, about 5 minutes
Add in garlic, stirring constantly for 1 minute
Add chicken, chicken broth and bay leaves, simmer for at least 1 ½ hours
30 minutes before serving, add in frozen veggies and noodles
Remove bay leaves, serve and enjoy!

Chicken Tortilla Soup

If you use chicken left over from making your broth, this is about as close as you can get to a "dump 'em all" soup recipe that gives you a nice little warm up when the cold winds blow. If you aren't using chicken left over from making broth, just cube five boneless skinless chicken breasts and saute in a Tablespoon of olive oil until chicken is no longer pink in the middle to start the soup, then pick up adding the garlic and cumin.

5 cups worth of chicken from making broth
2 cloves garlic, run through garlic press
1 teaspoon ground cumin
1 half gallon of chicken broth
2 packages (12 ounces each) frozen sweet corn
1 jar (24 ounces) chunky salsa, you pick the heat level
2 sweet onions, rough chop
Juice of 2 limes
1 $1/2$ teaspoon chili powder (recipe on page 160)
1 $1/2$ pounds corn tortilla chips
2 cups Monterey jack cheese, shredded (for topping)
1 bottle (minimum 12 ounce) squeeze sour cream (for topping)

In large pot over medium heat, combine chicken, garlic, and cumin, stir well
Add broth, corn, salsa, onions, lime juice, and chili powder
Bring to boil then reduce heat to low simmer
Simmer for at least an hour
Put tortilla chips in bowls and pour soup over chips
Top with cheese and sour cream
Enjoy as you warm up from the inside!

Cincinnati Style Chili

Closer to a sugo with chili spices, Cincinnati chili is served over pasta. Cincinnati chili is also referred to by the "ways", or the toppings added to it. Three way is pasta, chili, and cheese, four way adds either diced fresh onions or kidney beans, and five way includes both. You can always add sour cream, hot sauce, and/or oyster crackers, or really anything you want, because it's your dish, after all.

3 pounds ground chuck (80/20)
2 large sweet onions, diced, divided
3 cans (8 ounce) tomato sauce
$1/3$ cup chili powder (recipe on page 160)
2 cloves garlic, run through garlic press
1 $1/2$ teaspoons white vinegar
$1/2$ teaspoon cayenne pepper
$1/2$ teaspoon ground cinnamon
$1/2$ teaspoon worcestershire sauce
2 teaspoons salt (or to taste)
$1/2$ teaspoon ground black pepper to taste
1 $1/2$ pounds uncooked spaghetti
2 cups (8 ounces) cheddar cheese, shredded
1 $1/2$ cups red kidney beans
1 bag (16 ounce) oyster crackers (for topping)
1 bottle (minimum 12 ounce) squeeze sour cream (for topping)
1 jar (5 ounce minimum) hot sauce of choice (for topping)

Brown beef and onion in large pot over med-high heat
When beef is browned and onion is translucent, add tomato sauce, chili powder, garlic, vinegar, cayenne, cinnamon, and Worcestershire sauce
Simmer, uncovered, over low heat for at least 1 $1/2$ hours
About 20 minutes before serving, put pasta in a pot, cover with salted water
Bring to a boil, stir, turn off the heat, and cover
After 10 minutes, check if the pasta is done to your liking, drain pasta
Add salt and pepper to meat mix to taste
Serve with meat mixture over spaghetti, then top as desired

Colorado Green Chili

In Colorado and the Southwest, they like their chili green. You can buy three different kinds of chili peppers, roast them, add in tomatillos that you've roasted, and on and on, or you can do it the ~~lazy man's~~ easy way. You may not win a chili cookoff with this recipe, but you will put a darn good bowl of chili on the table with a minimum of effort. You can use leftover chicken from making broth, or sauté 3 diced boneless skinless chicken breasts in a Tablespoon of oil. Cubed, cooked pork is also a common ingredient instead of chicken. You can top however you like, things like diced avocado, fresh cilantro, shredded cheese, chopped onions, sour cream, crushed tortilla chips, let your imagination run free!

1 half gallon chicken broth
5 cups cooked chicken
2 cans (15 ounce) beans of choice (I use 1 great northern, 1 butter)
1 bottle (16 ounces) salsa verde (you decide the heat level)
2 teaspoons ground cumin
Toppings of choice

Combine all ingredients in a large pot
Bring to a boil, reduce to a simmer
Simmer for at least one hour
Serve with your toppings of choice and enjoy!

Italian Sausage Soup with Tortellini

This soup has almost all the things we Americans think of when we think of something Italian: sausage, garlic, tomatoes, basil, oregano, zucchini, pasta – what better way to warm up on a cold winter night? Serve with either a hearty Italian bread or the garlic bread from page 86.

2 pounds bulk sweet Italian sausage
2 carrots, sliced thin
1 large sweet onion, rough chop
3 cloves garlic, run through garlic press
1 half gallon chicken broth
2 boxes (750 grams, 26.46 ounces) Pomi® chopped tomatoes
1 can (8 ounce) tomato sauce
$^3/_4$ cup red wine
1 package (0.75 ounce) fresh basil, chiffonade cut
$^3/_4$ teaspoon dried oregano leaves
2 zucchini, cubed to about $^1/_2$" cubes
1 package (19 ounce) fresh cheese filled tortellini
1 bunch fresh parsley, chopped
Grated parmesan cheese (for topping)

In large pot, brown sausage, carrots, and onion until sausage is cooked, carrots are soft, and onion is translucent, about 8-10 minutes
Add in garlic, stirring constantly for one minute
Stir in broth, tomatoes, tomato sauce, wine, basil, and oregano
Bring to a boil, reduce to a simmer
Simmer uncovered for 30 minutes
Stir in zucchini and parsley, simmer covered for 30 minutes
Add tortellini for last 10 minutes
Serve, top with parmesan cheese, and mangia!

New England Clam Chowdah

If you have a particularly religious bunch your feeding on a Friday during Lent, or if you just have a hankering for some good old clam chowdah, this one will fit the bill.

1 pound bacon, diced
9 potatoes, peeled and cubed to about $^1/_2$" cubes
1 large sweet onion rough chop
3 Tablespoons all purpose flour
3 cups bottled clam juice
3 cups heavy whipping cream
3 cans (10 ounce) whole baby clams
1 Tablespoon salt (or to taste)
Ground black pepper to taste
1 bunch fresh parsley, chopped (for topping)
1 bag (16 ounce) oyster crackers (for topping)

In large pot over med-high heat, cook bacon until crisp, about 10 minutes
Remove bacon and drain on paper towels
Sauté potatoes and onion in bacon grease about 5 minutes
Sprinkle with flour and stir well to coat
Pour in clam juice, bring to a boil, reduce to simmer
Simmer until potatoes are tender, about 20 minutes
Add cream and clams, heat through
Serve with bacon, parsley, and oyster crackers; enjoy!

Popeye's Chicken Tortellini Soup

A certain make believe sailor used to get super strength from eating spinach, just in time to save the day. I'm not guaranteeing you'll get super strength, but you'll certainly have a belly full of energy to tackle whatever may come your way! As with my other soups, if you don't have chicken left over from making broth, you can sauté 4 cubed boneless skinless chicken breasts.

2 Tablespoons olive oil
5 carrots, sliced
5 ribs celery, sliced
1 large sweet onion, rough chop
3 cloves garlic, run through garlic press
4 pounds chicken from making broth
1 box (10 ounce) frozen spinach, unthawed
1 half gallon chicken broth
2 cans (10.75 ounce) cream of chicken soup
1 package (19 ounces) cheese tortellini
Grated parmesan cheese (for topping)
1 bag (16 ounce) oyster crackers (for topping)

In a large pot, sauté carrots in oil for 5 minutes, stirring occasionally
Add celery, cook for 5 minutes, stirring occasionally
Add onion, cook until soft, about 5 minutes, stirring occasionally
Add garlic, cook for one minute, stirring constantly
Add chicken and spinach, sauté until spinach thaws, then heats up
Add broth and cream of chicken
Heat through, then add tortellini
Simmer for 20 minutes
Serve with parmesan and oyster crackers for topping, and mangia!

Red Chili

If fire department cooks are known for anything, it's a steaming bowl of red. The first time I made this, some friends and I were going to a football game, and since I happened to not be working either of my jobs that day, and I enjoy cooking, I volunteered to cook some chili up. My wife got home just as my friends came to pick me up, and the bowl I gave her was proclaimed the best chili I ever made. My friends concurred (before they went overboard on the tailgating), so this is the recipe I use when I want to make red chili. If you want to make things easier, or you prefer the texture, you can brown up an equal amount of ground beef instead of dicing the chuck roast.

3 pounds chuck roast, cubed to about $^3/_8$" cubes
2 large sweet onions, rough chop
3 red bell peppers, rough chop
2 cloves garlic, run through garlic press
6 cans (10 ounce) canned Chili Fixins diced tomatoes
2 cans (15 ounce) tomato sauce
$^1/_3$ cup chili powder (see recipe on page 160)
2 bay leaves
1 teaspoon ground cumin
2 cans (16 ounces each) chili beans, undrained, you pick the heat level
2 cups (8 ounces) cheddar cheese, shredded (for topping)
Diced onion (for topping)
1 bottle (minimum 12 ounce) squeeze sour cream (for topping)

In large pot over med-high heat, combine beef, onions, peppers, and garlic
Stir occasionally, cook until beef is cooked through and peppers are tender
Drain excess fat
Add Chili Fixins, tomato sauce, chili powder, bay leaves, and cumin
Bring to a boil, reduce to simmer
Cover and simmer for at least 1 ½ hours, stirring occasionally
Stir in the beans, heat through
Serve with toppings and enjoy!

Split Pea with Ham Soup

Split pea with ham is one of those that takes me back to when I was a kid. Not necessary, but to shake things up a little, I use one pound green peas and one pound yellow peas. I have also made this soup with sausage instead of ham, because that's what we had left over from the previous day.

$^1/_2$ stick salted butter
3 carrots, diced
5 ribs celery, diced
1 large sweet onion, rough chop
4 cloves garlic, run through garlic press
$^1/_2$ gallon chicken broth
5 cups water
2 pounds ham, diced
2 pounds dried split peas
2 bay leaves
1 Tablespoon salt (or to taste)
1 teaspoon ground black pepper (or to taste)

Melt butter in large pot over med-low heat
Add carrots, cook for 5 minutes, stirring occasionally
Add celery, cook for 5 minutes, stirring occasionally
Add onion, cook for 5 minutes, stirring occasionally
Add garlic, cook for 1 minute, stirring constantly
Pour in chicken broth and water
Stir in ham, peas, and bay leaves
Bring to boil, then reduce to simmer
Simmer, stirring occasionally, until the peas are tender and the soup is thick, about 1 hour and 15 minutes
Season with salt and pepper to taste, then serve and enjoy!

Turkey Meatball Soup

You can make your own Italian turkey meatballs for this soup if you want, but I came up with this soup to be a quick weeknight meal for when I got home from the part time job, so I usually just buy premade Italian turkey meatballs. As with the chicken noodle soup, you can use whichever noodles you prefer, but you really owe it to you and your family to try Reames® noodles at some point.

2 Tablespoons salted butter
4 carrots, sliced
5 ribs celery, sliced
1 large sweet onion, rough chop
4 cloves garlic, run through garlic press
1 half gallon of prepared turkey broth
2 pounds ($^1/_2$ ounce size) Italian turkey meatballs
2 bay leaves
8 ounces frozen sweet corn
8 ounces frozen peas
8 ounces frozen green beans
1 package (16 ounce) Reames® noodles
1 Tablespoon salt (or to taste)
1 teaspoon ground black pepper (or to taste)
Grated parmesan cheese (for topping)
Italian croutons (for topping)

Melt butter in large pot over medium heat
Add in carrot slices, stirring occasionally, cook for 5 minutes
Add in celery slices, stirring occasionally, cook for 5 minutes
Add in onion, stirring occasionally, cook until just about soft, about 5 minutes
Add in garlic, stirring constantly for 1 minute
Add turkey broth, meatballs, and bay leaves, simmer for at least 1 ½ hours
30 minutes before serving, add in frozen veggies and noodles
Remove bay leaves, serve and enjoy!

White Chili

Is white chili true chili? Who cares? It's easy to make, it tastes good, that's all I care about. You can use chicken or turkey broth if you like, whichever one you happen to have handy when you make this. If you don't have chicken left over from making broth just use 5 cooked, cubed boneless skinless chicken breasts. Sometimes I split the beans and do a mix of great northern beans, butter beans, and cannellini (white kidney beans), it's your white chili, do what you like!

3 Tablespoons olive oil
2 large sweet onions, rough chop
4 cloves garlic, run through a garlic press
$1/2$ gallon chicken broth
6 cups chicken from making broth
3 cans (4 ounce) chopped green chile peppers, you pick the heat level
1 Tablespoon cayenne pepper
1 Tablespoon ground cumin
1 Tablespoon oregano
2 bay leaves
7 cans (14.5 ounces each) great northern beans, undrained
1 bottle (minimum 12 ounce) squeeze sour cream (for topping)
2 cups (8 ounces) Monterey jack cheese, shredded (for topping)

Heat the oil in a large pot over medium heat
Add onions, sauté until tender, about 10 minutes, stirring occasionally
Add garlic, sauté for 1 minute, stirring constantly
Add broth, chicken, peppers, cayenne, cumin, oregano, and bay leaves
Bring to a boil, then reduce to a simmer
Stir in beans, simmer until heated through, about 20-30 minutes
Serve with toppings desired and enjoy!

ARFF

ARFF stands for Aircraft Rescue and Firefighting. ARFF includes emergency response, mitigation, evacuation, and rescue of passengers and crew of aircraft involved in an accident or incident. Due to the large amount of people in a relatively small area, and the massive potential for fire from large amounts of aviation fuel, ARFF units need to be able to respond faster than traditional fire units. Traditional firefighting units are recommended to be able to reach any emergency in their area within six minutes. ARFF firefighters are required (not recommended) to be able to respond to any point on the airport that is the same distance as the midpoint of the furthest runway from their station within three minutes of the alarm for the first vehicle, and four minutes for all other vehicles. Airports may seem easy to get around since they have far less "streets" than city neighborhoods, but the perimeter roads, runways, and taxiways look far different than anything you might be used to seeing outside the airport fence. During an emergency, the driver of an ARFF apparatus must not only know where they're going and how to get there, they must also avoid any hazards along their path, including other vehicles and aircraft. Once it becomes dark out, the sea of different colored lights can be confusing if you're not used to it.

Like any firefighters, their first objective is to save the lives of those involved. This is accomplished by several means. Initially, ARFF units may provide an escape path through any fire for passengers and crew that are able to exit the plane. Other ARFF units will work towards extinguishing all other fire on the scene, including any fire that may be inside the aircraft. Any passengers or crew that are unable to exit the aircraft under their own power need to be removed from the aircraft. All passengers and crew involved need to be medically triaged, so the most severely injured with the highest chance of survival are treated and transported first. After the incident is stabilized, ARFF's main function is to preserve the scene for investigators to figure out what happened and how it happened, so it may be avoided in the future.

ARFF apparatus are designed very differently from structural fire apparatus. Although not an ideal circumstance, ARFF apparatus are designed so one firefighter can operate it by themselves. Since they must respond anywhere on the airport grounds, they must be able to travel off-road well. Since they are under the time constraints mentioned above, they must be relatively fast. This can be difficult to achieve, since they also must carry large quantities of water, sometimes as much as 4,500 gallons! They also have multiple mounted master stream nozzles, and some have articulating booms on top enabling them to provide an elevated stream if necessary. They also have to carry up to 500 pounds of chemicals for extinguishing combustible metal fires, since aircraft are mainly built of combustible metals. In addition to all of that, they must carry many of the things structural fire apparatus carry, such as extinguishers, hoselines, and rescue equipment.

The number and types of ARFF apparatus required for an airport is called it's index. The index is determined by the size and passenger capacity of the largest aircraft that uses the airport on a normal basis. Most airports that have passenger service are sized so one centrally located station can meet the response requirements. For a small airport that only receives planes shorter than 90 feet, there may only be one ARFF firefighter responding on one rig. Larger international airports can have multiple stations on airport grounds, with multiple apparatus at each station to be able to meet the requirements. The larger international airports will often have structural fire units stationed with the ARFF units, as well as specialty apparatus such as light towers, mass ventilation units, and movable stairways.

The training is intense for ARFF firefighters, both initial and ongoing. ARFF firefighters must be certified structural firefighters before becoming ARFF firefighters. After their initial training, every ARFF firefighter must recertify annually in 11 FAA mandated topics, ranging from airport layout to aircraft layout to firefighting operations. If a firefighter's training isn't up to date, that firefighter is not allowed to be assigned to ARFF apparatus. If they are, large fines can be levied against the airport.

Beef Dishes

Beef, or meat derived from cattle, is first divided into eight primal cuts. These are then broken down into 13 subprimals, which are then sliced or chopped into the steaks, roasts, and other cuts that we as consumers are more familiar with. Pretty much any way you can cook something can be used for some type of beef, but you need to use the proper form of cooking for the right cut of beef. Some excel with quick blasts of intense heat, such as grilling or broiling, while others are more suited for low and slow cooking. The more a cow uses a muscle, the leaner and tougher it will be. Conversely, the muscles that get used less are more marbled with fat, which makes them more tender. If you're ever unsure about how to select and then cook beef, go to a butcher shop and don't be shy about asking questions.

Beef Enchiladas

When you're on the hunt for an easy, quick, and delicious enchilada dinner, look no further than this recipe! If you prefer corn tortillas, by all means use them, but you will definitely find it easier to roll them if you heat them up first. For the cheese, I preferred the Mexican 4 cheese blend, but if you want to use another cheese go right ahead. Some other options include Monterey jack, pepper jack, cheddar – it's your dinner, use what you want. If you're feeling adventurous and want to dress up your enchiladas, after cooking you can garnish them with diced tomatoes, sliced green onions, pico de gallo – or not, these are very tasty and attractive without garnish as well.

3 pounds ground chuck (80/20)
2 medium sweet onions, diced
$1/4$ teaspoon garlic salt (or to taste)
$1/4$ teaspoon ground black pepper (or to taste)
2 cans (19 ounces each) enchilada sauce, divided
3 cups shredded Mexican 4 cheese blend, divided
12 (8 inch) flour tortillas

Preheat oven to 350F
Brown ground chuck and onions
Drain the ground chuck mixture
Season ground chuck mixture to taste with garlic salt and ground black pepper
Mix one cup of enchilada sauce and 2 cups of cheese into ground chuck mixture
Pour one can enchilada sauce in bottom of 9" x 13" casserole dish
Roll 1/12 of meat mixture into each tortilla and place seam side down in 9 x 13
Pour remaining enchilada sauce over enchiladas
Sprinkle remaining cheese over enchiladas
Bake until warmed through, 20-30 minutes
Serve and enjoy as your family says "Ole!"

Beef Stroganoff

Beef stroganoff (or Stroganov) dates back to the mid 1800s in Russia, where the chefs working for the Stroganov family first started making the dish we now recognize. Beef stroganoff is found (with geographic differences) worldwide. Here is the version I got from, well, not quite sure. It might have been from my Grandma, maybe from my Mom, or maybe from someone I worked with. Regardless of who it's from, if you recognize it as the same recipe you use, thank you!

3 pounds top round steak, cut into strips
$^1/_3$ cup vegetable oil, divided
2 large sweet onions, rough chop
1 pound button mushrooms, sliced
3 cans (10.75 ounces each) cream of mushroom soup
1 $^1/_2$ teaspoons paprika
12 ounces sour cream
1 $^1/_2$ pounds extra wide egg noodles, cooked

Heat half the oil in large pot over med-high heat
Cook beef strips until browned, about 10 minutes, stirring often
Remove beef and set aside
Add remaining oil, reduce heat to medium
Add onion, cook until tender, about 7-8 minutes, stirring occasionally
Add in mushrooms, cook until mushrooms are tender, about 5 minutes
Pour off fat
Add soup and paprika, heat to boil
Stir in sour cream and beef
Heat through, and serve over noodles
Enjoy!

Corned Beef Hash

Originally devised as a way to use leftovers, corned beef hash came into it's own a couple hundred years ago, when "Hash houses" popped up all over the US. Served for breakfast, it can be accompanied by eggs and toast. Served for lunch or dinner, it can be a side dish or entrée.

3 Tablespoons salted butter
3 Tablespoons olive oil
2 medium sweet onions, rough chop
2 pounds frozen southern style hash browns, thawed
3 pounds cooked corned beef, cubed
3 Tablespoons fresh parsley, chopped
$1/4$ teaspoon thyme
Pinch of salt, to taste
Pinch of ground black pepper, to taste

Melt butter in large skillet over medium heat, add olive oil
Add onion and cook until it's tender, about 10 minutes, stirring occasionally
Add hash browns, cook until tender, about 20 minutes, stirring occasionally
Stir in beef, parsley, and thyme
Cook until hash is crisp and browned, stirring often, about 15 minutes
Serve and enjoy!

Country Fried Steak

The American creation known as country (or chicken) fried steak traces back to the mid 1800s when European immigrants to Texas used local ingredients to make their recipes for wiener schnitzel. Country fried steak can be served for any meal, with breakfast including eggs, hash browns, and toast, while lunch and dinner often have mashed potatoes, vegetables, and biscuits on the side. As you cook the steaks, you can keep the previously cooked ones on a baking sheet in a 170F oven to keep them hot while cooking the rest.

6 (8 ounce) cube steaks
1 $\frac{1}{2}$ teaspoons salt, divided
2 Tablespoons ground black pepper, divided
3 cups all purpose flour
6 eggs, beaten
1 cup vegetable oil
2 Tablespoons butter
3 cups whole milk

Season meat on both sides with salt and pepper
Dredge each steak in flour, dip in egg, then flour again
Heat oil in large cast iron skillet over med-high heat to 350F
Fry steaks until golden brown, 3-4 minutes per side
Drain on paper towels, hold in oven
After cooking all of the steaks, pour off the vegetable oil
Over medium heat, melt butter
Whisk in 2 Tablespoons of the dredging flour, scraping up any bits on the bottom
Cook for one minute, stirring constantly
Gradually whisk in milk
Cook until thickened and bubbly, 5 more minutes, stirring frequently
Add salt and pepper to taste, gravy should be rather peppery
Serve, covering steaks with gravy
Enjoy!

F's Famous Corned Beef

Every year, my wife Heather and I host a St. Patrick's Day party, where we serve my corned beef. Even people who normally don't like corned beef like my buttery brisket. It's important to simmer only hot enough that steam comes off the top of the water, boiling makes the meat tough and stringy. I developed my technique after the first time I made corned beef for our party. I boiled it, chilled it, and then reheated the whole amount in a slow cooker. The meat was tough and stringy, but when I reheated it in the microwave the next day, it was better! I had found out about simmering instead of boiling by the next party, and I figured if it was better after reheating it, why not reheat it before serving it the first time?

Point cut corned beef brisket – 1 pound per person
Pickling spice
Irish dry stout beer
Loaf of rye bread
Sliced swiss cheese
Jar of mustard of choice

In large pot, place corned beef and fill with water
Remove corned beef, add seasoning packet(s) included with meat
Bring to a boil, then add the beef back in
Bring to a simmer, then simmer for one hour per pound of biggest brisket
When done, remove beef from pot and refrigerate overnight in sealed container
The next day, remove beef from container, scrape surface fat off
Place beef in pot, fill with water
Remove corned beef, add the same amount of pickling spice as 1st day
Repeat day one, boil, add beef, simmer, refrigerate
The next day, remove beef from container, scrape surface fat off
Slice beef thin, place rack in either covered roaster or electric roaster
Fill bottom of roaster with beer, keep below level of rack
Place cooked, sliced corned beef on top of rack, with lid on, reheat at 200F for about an hour
Serve and enjoy!

Pot Roast

Pot roast is an easy, flavorful meal that can be cooked many ways. I prefer using a covered roasting pan in the oven or an electric roaster. It can also be done on the stovetop in a dutch oven or in a slow cooker. You can use whatever veggies you want in the roaster, if there's one I mention that you don't like, by all means don't use it! If you choose to turn it down to 200F after cooking to hold, it will really amp up the tenderness of the meat.

2 Tablespoons vegetable oil
4 $^1/_2$ pounds chuck roast
4 garlic cloves, peeled and halved lengthwise
4 Tablespoons season salt
1 Tablespoon ground black pepper
1 can or bottle dark beer
3 pounds potatoes, cut into about 1" cubes
3 medium sweet onions, quartered
1 pound baby carrots
1 pound button mushrooms

Heat vegetable oil in heavy skillet over med-high heat
Cut slits in roasts(s) and stuff garlic into meat
Coat outside of roast(s) with season salt and pepper
Sear all sides of roast(s), set meat aside
Deglaze skillet with dark beer, scraping any bits off the bottom
Pour beer into bottom of roaster
Place potatoes, onions, and carrots on bottom of roaster in deglazing liquid
Place beef on top of veggies
Place mushrooms on and around roast(s)
Cook , covered, at 350F for one hour per pound of biggest roast
You can serve after this, or turn heat down to 200F and hold until ready to serve
To serve, remove meat from roaster, slice across the grain
Enjoy the yum!

Prime Rib

Cooking a prime rib can be daunting for the first time. For most people it is the most they have ever spent on food, and it's usually for a special occasion so lots of people will be there. I have found the reverse sear is the easiest way to cook prime rib. It's exactly as it sounds – you cook it first and sear it last, the reverse of what you would expect. Dry brining overnight helps amp up the flavor, also.

7 pound bone in standing rib roast
2 Tablespoons kosher salt
$^3/_4$ stick salted butter, softened
2 Tablespoons fresh rosemary, chopped
1 Tablespoon fresh thyme, chopped
1 teaspoon ground black pepper

Cover roast generously with kosher salt, refrigerate overnight
Mix butter, rosemary, thyme, and pepper in a small bowl
Spread butter mixture over roast, place in large covered roasting pan fat cap up
Cook until center of roast reads 125F on an instant read thermometer, about 3 $^1/_2$ to 4 hours
Remove roast from oven, keep covered
Increase oven temperature to highest possible, 500F – 550F
Remove cover of roasting pan, place back in oven for 6-10 minutes
Remove from oven, carve, and serve immediately
After cleaning, find the nearest comfy chair and enjoy your meat coma!

Reuben Sandwiches

Much the same as corned beef hash, reuben sandwiches are a great way to use leftover corned beef. There are many accounts of the creation of the reuben, and any or all of them may be true. Without time travel, we'll never know.   The traditional sandwich includes corned beef, swiss cheese, sauerkraut, and Russian dressing grilled between two slices of rye bread. There are many variations, including the one below that uses thousand island dressing in place of the Russian dressing. As in other recipes, sandwiches that are finished can rest in a 170F oven on a baking sheet while cooking the rest of the sandwiches.

Softened butter or mayonnaise
12 slices rye bread
12 slices leftover corned beef
12 slices swiss cheese
1 $^1/_2$ cups sauerkraut, drained
$^3/_4$ cup thousand island dressing

Preheat a large skillet or griddle over medium heat
Spread butter or mayonnaise on one side of bread slices
On half of the bread slices, spread the plain side with thousand island dressing
Lay a slice of swiss cheese on the dressing, then 2 slices corned beef, 1/6th of the sauerkraut, and another slice of swiss cheese
Top with the remaining bread, plain side in
Grill sandwiches until both sides are golden brown and the cheese melts, about 5-6 minutes per side
Serve and enjoy!

Rileyburgers

I came up with this after our family ate at one of our favorite local restaurants. I ordered grilled onions on my burger, and they came out as a slice of an onion, grilled right next to the burger patty. They had a portabella burger on the menu for vegetarians. I thought how good it would taste to put a portabella cap on with the grilled onion. And what goes with beef, mushrooms, and onions? Swiss cheese, of course! Then a few years later our local grocery store got pretzel buns in the bread aisle. It took a few years, but the Rileyburger was complete.

2 pounds ground chuck (80/20)
Pinch of salt, to taste
Pinch of ground black pepper, to taste
2 large sweet onions
6 portabella mushroom caps
6 slices swiss cheese
6 pretzel hamburger buns

Split the beef into 6 equal patties
Generously sprinkle salt and pepper on both sides of the patties
Slice the onions into about ½" slices
Remove the mushroom stems
Under cold running water gently scrape the gills off the undersides of the caps
Preheat a grill to medium heat
Put the burgers, onions, and mushroom caps on the grill
Cook all until done to your liking
Put swiss cheese on burger patties and toast buns on grill
Serve and enjoy!

Shepherd's Pie

Shepherd's pie originated hundreds of years ago as, you guessed it, a way to use leftovers. In its earliest iterations, the pie dish was lined on the bottom and sides with potatoes, as well as the top. As with many of today's recipes, shepherd's pie has gone from getting rid of leftovers to a dish created on its own for a meal. The recipe may seem like it's bouncing around a bit, but you're cooking the other part of the dish during what would normally be down time while the first part is cooking.

2 pounds red skin potatoes, cubed to about 1" cubes
2 pounds ground chuck (80/20)
1 Tablespoon basil
1 tablespoon rosemary
1 package (12 ounces) frozen carrots and peas
1 package dry brown gravy mix
$1/2$ cup milk
$1/2$ stick salted butter
1 cup cheddar cheese, finely shredded
Pinch of salt, to taste
Pinch of ground black pepper, to taste
Sprinkling of paprika to garnish

Boil the potatoes in salted water until tender, about 30 minutes
Preheat oven to 350F
While potatoes are boiling, brown ground chuck with basil and rosemary
Make gravy according to directions
When beef is browned, mix gravy in (mixture should be fairly dry)
Cook beef mixture over medium flame for 10 minutes
Rinse potatoes with cold water in colander, return boiling pot
Add milk and butter to potatoes, mash potatoes with potato masher
Add salt and pepper to beef mixture to taste
Pour beef mixture into 9"x13" casserole dish, cover with mashed potatoes
Sprinkle paprika lightly over potatoes
Cook in oven for 30 minutes, sprinkling cheese on top for last 5 minutes
As the Irish would say, Slainte!

Stuffed Bell Peppers

Virtually every society that has access to peppers has some form of stuffed peppers in their cuisine. From Spain's pimientos rellenos to the central Asian dolma, Mexico's chile relleno to Lithuania's kimsti pipirai, some form of stuffed peppers is enjoyed just about everywhere.

12 bell peppers, tops and seeds removed
2 pounds ground chuck (80/20)
3 celery ribs, sliced thin
1 $^1/_2$ medium sweet onion, diced
3 cups cooked rice
2 cans (15 ounce) tomato sauce, divided
Pinch of salt, to taste
Pinch of ground black pepper to taste
2 cups (8 ounces) mozzarella cheese, shredded

Preheat oven to 375F
Bring a large pot of water to a boil
Cook bell peppers in water until soft, 6-8 minutes, drain
Brown ground beef and celery over med-high heat until done, 7-10 minutes
After about 5 minutes, add the onions
After draining the grease, transfer beef mixture to a large bowl
Mix beef mixture, rice, and 1 can tomato sauce with beef
Season mix with salt and pepper to taste
Stuff bell peppers with beef mixture
Arrange stuffed peppers in a baking dish
Add enough water to baking dish to end up about 1" deep
Pour other can of tomato sauce over the peppers
Cook until heated through, about 30 minutes, sprinkling tops with cheese for last 5 minutes
Serve and enjoy!

Brush Trucks

Brush trucks are designed mainly for fighting wildland fires. They can range anywhere from a "homemade" version on a 4x4 pickup truck chassis to factory built on vehicles such as a Hummer or light truck chassis. Almost always four wheel drive, they generally will carry a small water tank and pump, a small amount of hose that is often stored on a reel, along with equipment specifically for wildland firefighting, such as corn brooms, shovels, etc...

Brush trucks usually have truck mounted nozzles for applying water while the firefighters are safely inside the vehicle. This requires the use of a pump that is able to pump water while the vehicle is moving, which most structural fire engines do not have.

Specifications for brush trucks vary widely. Some are made for use in wide open fields and can be larger, while others are most often utilized in mountain forests where light weight and maximum maneuverability are valuable. Some also do double duty as mini-pumpers for the structural firefighting side of things, meaning they must be able to carry more firefighters, more water, more hose, and more equipment.

Pork Dishes

Pork is defined as the meat from a domestic pig, as opposed to the wild boar that a domesticated pig descended from. Pork is the most commonly consumed meat in the world, with evidence of pigs being domesticated dating back to 13000BC in Mesopotamia. With the exception of Jewish and Muslim societies, pork is eaten by all cultures. Pork can be eaten freshly cooked or preserved. Pork chops, pork steaks, tenderloins, ribs all represent the freshly cooked – sausage, ham, and everybody's favorite bacon are just some of the examples of preserved pork dishes. With such a variety of the base, the options for what to cook using the various pork products is pretty endless.

Years ago, pork was always cooked to well done to kill the parasite that causes trichinosis. Some even believed that eating applesauce along with your pork killed the parasite. According to the USDA, neither is necessary anymore. Improved feeding practices and high levels of biosecurity and hygiene have taken the number of cases down to an average of 16 cases per year (with most of those being traced to eating wild game) in the United States. Considering we in the US eat an average of nine million metric tons of pork every year, 16 cases is pretty insignificant. Pork done medium rare can be every bit as good as beef done medium rare, and nowadays can be done just as safely.

Bangers and Mash

Bangers is the UK/Irish term for breakfast sausage, dating back to WWI, when meat rationing drove the water content in sausages so high that they were just as likely to pop as be cooked properly. Nowadays, you can find bangers and mash on menus from breakfast only places to gastropubs. On our first trip to Ireland, I had the most amazing bangers and mash at The Front Door/Sonny Molloy's in Galway. Ever since that day I have tried to duplicate that dish, and here is the closest I have come. I think maybe it tasted a little better since I was on vacation, and it was my first time in Ireland, or at least that's what I keep telling myself…

12 links pork sausage (bangers if you can get them, otherwise bratwurst)
4 large sweet onions, sliced
5 pounds red skin potatoes, cubed
$^3/_4$ stick salted butter, divided
Salt and ground black pepper to taste
$^1/_2$ gallon chicken broth
1 bottle red wine
$^1/_3$ cup milk
1 Tablespoon dry mustard powder

Preheat oven to 170F
Cook sausage in skillet over medium heat until browned, about 5 minutes per side
While sausages are cooking, boil potatoes until tender, about 30 minutes
When sausages are done, put in oven safe dish and let rest in oven
Deglaze pan with a cup of red wine, scraping all the bits off the bottom
Add 3 Tablespoons butter, caramelize onions over low heat
When onions are caramelized, add rest of wine and chicken broth
Boil mixture until about half it's volume, about 15 minutes
Drain potatoes when tender, rinse with cold water
Return potatoes to boiling pot, add rest of butter, milk, and mustard powder
Mash potatoes until smooth
Serve with sausage on top of potatoes, covered with gravy
Dream of overseas and enjoy!

Biscuits and Gravy

I grew up loving biscuits and gravy, because the only time I got to have it was when we would go out to eat at a southern based chain for breakfast when we were leaving for vacation. I loved their biscuits and gravy, until I grew up and had real biscuits and gravy at a locally owned Mom and Pop greasy spoon that half the time you had to duck as Mom and Pop were throwing things at each other as they argued across the restaurant. I then branched out and honed in on how I liked my biscuits and gravy. I discovered that I like a sweet and heat mix, and when I had breakfast at Butler's Pantry in Stowe, VT., I discovered the last link in the chain of the ultimate biscuits and gravy.

3 pounds maple breakfast sausage
1 large sweet onion, diced
1 pound button mushrooms, sliced
$^1/_2$ stick salted butter, divided
1 clove garlic, run through garlic press
1 $^1/_2$ Tablespoon rosemary
2 cups baking mix
$^1/_2$ cup grated parmesan cheese
5 $^2/_3$ cups whole milk, divided
$^3/_4$ cup all purpose flour
Ground black pepper, crushed red pepper, salt, and maple syrup to taste

Preheat oven to 400F
Brown sausage, onion, and mushroom in large pot
Stir flour into sausage mixture until fully mixed
Gradually stir in 5 cups milk
Cook gravy until thickness is what you like, add salt, black pepper, red pepper, and maple syrup to taste
While gravy thickens, melt 3 Tablespoons butter in small pan
Sauté garlic in butter one minute, then remove from heat and add rosemary
Combine garlic butter with baking mix and parmesan
Stir in $^2/_3$ cup milk, drop batter on to baking sheet, bake for 10 minutes
Brush biscuits with melted butter, bake until lightly browned on bottom, about 5 more minutes, serve with gravy covering biscuits, and enjoy!

Haluski

Haluski is based on a traditional Polish dish, adapted for what was available in the New World. Today, you will find Haluski in many old time restaurants in Pittsburgh, but since I discovered it, you will also find it in your kitchen if you follow my recipe.

$^1/_2$ pound bacon, chopped
3 pounds Polish sausage (fresh, not smoked)
1 large sweet onion, rough chop
2 cloves garlic, run through garlic press
1 large head green cabbage, cored and rough chop
1 Tablespoon season salt
1 teaspoon ground black pepper
$^1/_2$ teaspoon garlic powder
$^1/_2$ teaspoon onion powder
$^1/_4$ teaspoon paprika
2 pounds wide egg noodles

Cook bacon in large stock pot over med-high heat until crispy, about 10 minutes
Put Polish sausage in pot filled with water, simmer (not boil) for 45 minutes
Add onion, cook until caramelized, stirring constantly, about 10 minutes
Add garlic, stir a few times to mix into the bacon and onion
Add cabbage, cook for 10 minutes, stirring occasionally
Add salt, pepper, garlic and onion powders, and paprika
Reduce heat to low and cover
Cook for 30 minutes, stirring occasionally
Put pasta in a pot, cover with salted water
Bring to a boil
Stir, turn off the heat, and cover
After 10 minutes, check if the pasta is done to your liking
Drain, add pasta and sausage to cabbage
Serve and think of the old country!

Jambalaya

Jambalaya came about through West African, French, Spanish, and Native American influences. There are as many types of jambalaya as cooks in Louisiana. Meat, vegetables, rice all cooked together, and you have jambalaya. You can use any type of sausage you want, you can use chicken left over from making broth or not, you can use tomatoes or replace the liquid with something else, you can skip the shrimp, it's your jambalaya, take my recipe and make it your own!

2 Tablespoons olive oil
1 pound andouille sausage, cut into $^1/_4$" slices
2 medium sweet onions, rough chop
3 bell peppers, chopped
5 ribs celery, chopped
$^1/_2$ teaspoon salt (or to taste)
1 teaspoon cajun seasoning (recipe on page 158)
2 cups uncooked white rice
2 cans (14.5 ounces each) diced tomatoes with juice
3 cloves garlic, run through garlic press
3 cups chicken broth
4 bay leaves
$^1/_4$ teaspoon thyme
2 pounds cooked chicken from making broth, roughly shredded
2 pounds peeled and deveined raw shrimp

Heat olive oil in large pot, stir in sausage and cook for 2 minutes
Add onion, bell pepper, celery, salt, and cajun seasoning
Cook, stirring occasionally, until vegetables are soft, about 10 minutes
Stir in rice until evenly mixed with vegetable mixture
Add in tomatoes with juice, garlic, chicken broth, bay leaves, and thyme
Bring to a simmer over med-high heat, then back heat down to med-low
Simmer for 20 minutes, covered
Add chicken and shrimp, cook uncovered until shrimp turn pink, about 10 minutes
Take pot off stove, let rest for 5 minutes, then laissez les bons temps rouler!

Mushroom Pork Chops

Looking for an easy way to make some pork chops that are not only full of flavor, but moist as all get out? Here you go! These go well with either mashed potatoes or wild rice.

6 (1 $\frac{1}{4}$ inch thick) pork chops
Salt to taste
Ground black pepper to taste
2 Tablespoons salted butter
1 pound sliced mushrooms
1 cup milk
2 cans (10.75 ounce) cream of mushroom soup

Preheat oven to 350F
Season both sides of chops with salt and pepper
Melt butter in large skillet over med-high heat
Sear both sides of chops in the butter, about 3-4 minutes per side
Place the chops in a 9" x 13" casserole dish
Add mushrooms to skillet you just pulled the chops from, reduce heat to medium
Stir occasionally until soft, about 5 minutes
In separate mixing bowl, combine the milk with the soup
Cover pork chops with mushrooms and soup mixture
Cook until chops are done to your liking
Minimum temperature you want your pork is medium rare, which is 145F - 150F
Medium is 150F – 155F, medium well is 155F – 160F, and well is 160F +
Serve with your favorite sides, and try not to eat like a pig!

Pork and Kraut

There are times when plans are already in place for the workday that simply must be worked around by the cook. This recipe is one that's quick to put together, and hands off for the entire cooking time. If you have the time, sear the pork on all sides to caramelize the outside, but if you don't have the time, the pork still comes out awesome. It can be made in a covered roasting pan in the oven, or in an electric roasting pan. Because of the sauerkraut, it does have a unique aroma while cooking, but have faith – it comes out delicious. One time while making this at the station, four guys in a row came through the kitchen and commented on the smell, asking if the previous shift had forgotten to take the garbage out. Then the last remaining crewmember (the one well known for eating anything and everything) came through the kitchen and made a big production about how good it smelled!

2 pounds sauerkraut of choice
1 sweet onion, sliced thin
2 (3 ounces each) packages pork flavored ramen noodles
4 $^1/_2$ pounds pork country ribs (or boneless pork rib ends)
Salt to taste
Ground black pepper to taste
3 pounds baby red skin potatoes, washed and quartered
2 pounds baby carrots

Preheat oven to 400F
In bottom of roasting pan, mix sauerkraut, onion, and broken ramen noodles
Sprinkle seasoning packets from ramen over mixture
Season pork with salt and pepper, sear if desired
Place pork, potatoes, and carrots on sauerkraut mixture
Cover, cook until pork is 165F and potatoes and carrots are soft
Serve and enjoy!

Pork Schnitzel

Schnitzel is defined as a thin slice of meat fried in fat. Almost every world culture has a version, with the most well known being the wiener schnitzel originally from Vienna, Austria. The original must be made with veal, but any meat may be pounded thin, breaded, and fried. The recipe here calls for pork, but you can use chicken if you like. I also went with the baked or oven-fried version, because no matter what you did, the smell of the oil hung around the station for a couple days after cooking, so I tried not to subject the other two shifts to that smell when they didn't get to enjoy the food that left it.

2 Tablespoons olive oil, divided
6 boneless pork chops, pounded to about $1/4$" thick
Pinch of salt on each side of each chop
Pinch of ground black pepper on each side of each chop
$3/4$ cup all purpose flour
1 Tablespoon paprika
2 eggs, beaten
2 cups seasoned bread crumbs
Zest of one large lemon

Preheat oven to 425F
Line large baking sheet with foil and drizzle half of olive oil on foil
Salt and pepper both sides of each piece of pork
Mix flour and paprika in a pie tin, beat eggs in a shallow bowl
Mix bread crumbs and lemon zest in another pie tin
Place baking sheet in preheated oven
Set up an assembly line with the flour mixture, the eggs, and bread crumbs
Dredge each piece in flour mixture, then egg, then bread crumbs
Place each piece on a clean plate, in one layer after breading
Take baking sheet out of oven and place all pieces on it
Drizzle other half of olive oil over pieces, Bake for 5-6 minutes
Flip pieces, bake until meat is 145F, about 5-6 more minutes
Serve with your favorite side dish, and Prost!

Pulled Pork

Pulled pork is a great one to pull (get it?) out when you have to feed a crowd on a budget. Even in 2020, pork shoulder roast can usually be had for less than $2.00 per pound, so even figuring $^3/_4$ pound per person you're looking at less than $10.00 invested in the protein. If you don't have access to apple flavored beer, you can always just use apple juice or cider for the liquid under the rack. You can use whatever bun you like to hold the goodness, I was always partial to onion rolls.

4 $^1/_2$ pound pork shoulder roast
$^1/_4$ cup season salt
2 Tablespoons ground black pepper
1 cup brown sugar
2 cans apple flavored beer
12 buns of choice
Barbecue sauce of choice
Cole slaw (recipe on page 79) for topping

Preheat oven to 350F
Rub season salt and black pepper all over roast
Pack brown sugar all over roast
In a covered roasting pan, pour beer on bottom of pan and place rack in pan
Place roast on rack
Put cover on pan
Cook for 1 hour per pound at 350F
When cooking time is done, don't open oven, turn temperature down to 200F
Hold at 200F until time to serve, the longer you cook at 200F, the more tender the meat ends up
Pull pan from oven when ready to serve
Pull meat into shreds
Serve and get some barbecue in ya!

Stromboli

A stromboli is dough wrapped around cheese and meat into a turnover type dish. Like many foods, depending on who you ask, you get different stories as to who invented it. Stromboli differ from calzones in both the shape (calzones are just folded in half, stromboli are rolled) and the filling (calzones include sauce inside, stromboli generally do not). Since stromboli is basically rolled pizza, use your favorite toppings inside - customize the recipe below however you want. As with other recipes made on a baking sheet, use non-stick foil, or parchment paper, or use non-stick cooking spray on the baking sheet to prevent sticking.

1 pound sweet Italian sausage
1 large sweet onion, diced
8 ounces button mushrooms, sliced
2 cans (13.8 ounces each) refrigerated pizza dough
2 cups (8 ounces) mozzarella cheese, shredded
$^1/_2$ stick melted butter
1 clove garlic, run through garlic press
Grated parmesan cheese, for topping
6 cups warmed pizza sauce, for dipping (1 cup per person)

Preheat oven to 400F
Brown sausage and onion in skillet, about 7-10 minutes
Add mushrooms for last 2 minutes of sausage browning
When mixture is done, drain and set aside
Unroll dough on a lightly floured surface
Press out dough until each is about 10" x 14", transfer dough to baking sheet
Sprinkle half of the cheese on each crust, leaving 1" around all edges
Spread the sausage mixture on top of the cheese
Fold the short edges of the dough over the filling,
Roll each dough from long edge and leave the seam down
Mix garlic into butter, brush on outside, sprinkle with parmesan
Bake until outside is golden brown, about 30 minutes
Slice ($^1/_3$ of a stromboli will feed a hungry firefighter), serve, and enjoy!

Chief's Buggy

A term that dates back to the beginning of the fire service in America, the Chief's Buggy is still used today. In the early days of the fire service in America, the apparatus was either hand pulled or pulled by horses. Regardless of which method the apparatus used to respond to fires, the Chief would have a horse drawn buggy to transport them. These early buggies carried the Chief, sometimes an assistant, and very little else. Modern Chief's buggies range from sedans similar to police cars to full size SUVs, along with everything else in between. Traditionally, the administrative Chiefs drive unmarked vehicles, which may or may not have emergency light and siren packages. The line Chiefs that run the day to day operations, as well as any fireground operations, generally will be in marked vehicles with full emergency light and siren packages.

Today's line Chief buggies carry much more than a Chief. Often housed in full size SUVs, in the rear cargo area can be found command centers, small extra equipment for the companies under their command, disaster supplies, sometimes even medical equipment if the Chief is expected to respond to those type of calls. Since it is not unusual for a Chief to spend a good portion of their day on the road, and the people in that position are some of the highest ranking members of the department, comfort can be very important. Not so long ago, most Engines and Ladders had open rear cabs, exposing the firefighters to the elements, and the enclosed front portion of the cab lacked creature comforts such as air conditioning, power windows, intermittent wipers, or even heat besides windshield defrosters – Chiefs buggies had those and more. Even the busiest of fire companies spent less time in their apparatus than a line Chief, however.

Some departments have a Driver assigned to the line Chiefs, with the Driver acting as an assistant to the Chief on larger incidents and being assigned to one of the fire companies on smaller incidents, like a conventional house fire. In the departments that have this, that is a premium position that can be highly sought after.

Poultry Dishes

Poultry is defined as domesticated birds kept by humans for their eggs, meat, or feathers. It is the second most common meat source in the world, owing to the selective breeding done over centuries. This selective breeding favored birds that grew faster, laid eggs more reliably, and had bigger breasts.

Poultry must be cooked thoroughly to eliminate the risk of foodborne illness. To keep things simple, the USDA recommends all meat be cooked to 165F for 30 seconds. The problem is, white meat cooked to 165F has a very dry texture. The safety depends on both the temperature and the time at temperature, so by extending the time, you can lower the temperature. For white meat, moisture and texture wise, the ideal temperature is 145F to 150F. By holding a breast to a temperature of 145F for 8 minutes and 24 seconds, or 150F for 2 minutes and 42 seconds, you can have a much more enjoyable eating experience with the same safety. Dark meat is safe at the same temperature/time combinations, but you actually want to exceed the temperature with dark meat, since it needs to be 175F to 180F for the connective tissue to break down into gelatin and make the meat tender and juicy as opposed to chewy and rubbery. As long as it's cooked properly, the main food safety issue is from cross contamination during preparation. Studies have shown that rinsing poultry in the sink spreads far more bacteria throughout the kitchen than it removes from the bird, leading experts to recommend against the practice.

One of the things that cooks do to help with the moisture level in white meat is to brine the bird before cooking. J. Kenji Lopez-Alt on the seriouseats.com website takes a "Mythbusters" approach to cooking, and has some excellent articles on brining. To very briefly summarize, dry brining gives you moist, flavorful poultry. In contrast, wet brining gives you moist, flavorless poultry. Wet brining with other flavoring ingredients in addition to the salt offers no advantage to flavor, since the flavor molecules are generally too big to penetrate the cell membranes.

Chicken Cordon Bleu

The origins of cordon bleu date back to the late 1940s. In what is probably a case of not letting the truth get in the way of a good story, it was created by a chef at a restaurant that had two large parties show up saying they had reservations, but the restaurant only had a reservation for one of the parties. To stretch the ingredients, the enterprising chef butterflied the chicken breasts she had, filled them with ham and cheese, then breaded and fried them. The owner offered the chef a cordon bleu, or blue ribbon, signifying an excellent cook. The modest chef declined the blue ribbon, but said that would be a good name for the dish. As with other recipes made on a baking sheet, use non-stick foil, or parchment paper, or use non-stick cooking spray on the baking sheet to prevent sticking. Variations abound for this recipe – you can use pepperoni and mozzarella cheese for an Italian flair, sliced mushrooms instead of the ham, spinach and your choice of cheese, whatever you like! If you want to remove some of the calories, you can skip the bread crumbs if you like.

6 boneless, skinless chicken breasts
$1/2$ teaspoon salt
$1/4$ teaspoon ground black pepper
9 slices swiss cheese
$3/4$ pound shaved ham lunchmeat
1 cup seasoned panko bread crumbs

Preheat oven to 350F with baking sheet in oven
Pound chicken breasts to $1/4$" thickness
Sprinkle salt and pepper on both sides of chicken
Place $1/6$ of the ham on each piece of chicken
Place 1 slice of cheese on each piece of chicken
Roll each piece of chicken tightly and secure with a toothpick
Place seam side down on baking sheet, coat chicken evenly with bread crumbs
Bake 35 minutes, covering each piece with $1/2$ slice of cheese for last 5 minutes
Remove toothpicks, serve and enjoy!

Chicken "Enchidalas"

First, the spelling. When my kids were little, one of them had problems pronouncing enchiladas, coming out enchidalas instead. The name stuck, so that's what I call them. The definition of an enchilada is a rolled tortilla stuffed with meat and covered with a sauce. Enchiladas date back to at least Aztec times (starting around 1300AD) with people that had easy access to seafood wrapping tortillas around small fish. Later, as street food, they were merely tortillas dipped into sauce and eaten without fillings. Modern day iterations have amped up the filling, including cheese, beans, rice, potatoes, vegetables, and even eggs in the middle of the rolled tortillas.

2 cans (10.75 ounces each) cream of chicken soup
16 ounces sour cream
16 ounces pico de gallo or chunky salsa (you pick the heat level)
1 Tablespoon and 1 teaspoon chili powder (recipe on page 160)
3 boneless skinless chicken breasts, cooked and chopped
3 cups (12 ounces) shredded Mexican 4 cheese blend, divided
12 flour tortillas, soft taco size
1 bunch green onions, sliced (for garnish)

Preheat oven to 350F
Spray insides of two 9" x 13" casserole dishes with non-stick cooking spray
In a large bowl, mix soup, sour cream, pico de gallo or salsa, and chili powder
Remove 2 cups of mixture into another bowl, mix in chicken and 2 cups cheese
Divide chicken mixture into quarters, then spread $1/3$ of each quarter down the middle of each tortilla
Roll up each tortilla and place 6 in each casserole dish, seam side down
Spread remaining soup mixture over tops of enchidalas
Bake 40 minutes, sprinkling rest of cheese over tops for last 5 minutes
Garnish with sliced green onions
Serve with toppings of choice, and exclaim "Buen provecho!" (Bon appetit!)

Conference Call Chicken Pot Pie

Pot pie traditionally is made in individual servings, and has both a top and bottom crust. When making at the firehouse, we didn't have enough oven safe individual size dishes, so I would forgo the bottom crust to make it easier to cook in such large amounts. Trust me, you'll never miss it. Oh, and the conference call thing – I was on a conference call and gathering the items for making pot pie. I thought I was on mute, and trying to hold the phone while getting the cream of chicken soup out of the pantry I dropped the cans on the floor. Knowing how much I enjoy drinking beer, I immediately got called out for drinking while on the call and no one would believe me that it was cans of soup!

1 Tablespoon vegetable oil
5 carrots, sliced
5 ribs celery, sliced
1 large sweet onion, rough chop
6 boneless skinless chicken breasts, cooked and cubed
1 bag (12 ounce) frozen green beans
1 bag (12 ounce) frozen peas
1 bag (12 ounce) frozen sweet corn
2 cans cream of chicken soup – (1) 22.6 ounce, (1) 10.5 ounce
3 cups baking mix
1 $\frac{1}{2}$ cups milk
3 eggs, beaten

Sauté carrots, celery, and onions in oil over medium flame until soft
Preheat oven to 400F
Mix sauteed veggies, chicken, frozen veggies, and soup in large bowl
Spray bottom half of covered roasting pan with non-stick cooking spray
Pour veggie/chicken/soup mixture into bottom half of covered roasting pan
Mix baking mix, milk, and eggs in bowl, pour over top of mixture in pan
Bake until golden brown, about 40 minutes
Serve and enjoy a taste of childhood!

Lasagna Alfredo

Lasagna has been called spaghetti flavored cake, so why not make a fettucine alfredo with chicken flavored cake? This recipe is big enough to fill two separate 9" x 13" casserole dishes or the bottom half of a covered roasting pan. Although since we're not using the top of the pan to cover it, can I just call it a roasting pan?

6 cups ricotta cheese
2 packages (10 ounces each) frozen chopped spinach, thawed and drained
5 boneless skinless chicken breasts, cooked and cubed
3 jars (16 ounces each) prepared Alfredo sauce of choice, divided
2 packages no boil lasagna noodles
6 cups (24 ounces) mozzarella cheese, shredded, divided

Preheat oven to 350F
In large bowl, mix chicken and 1 jar Alfredo sauce
In separate bowl, mix ricotta and spinach
Pour half of one jar of Alfredo sauce on bottom of each casserole dish (or whole jar on bottom of roasting pan)
Place layer of lasagna noodles
Cover noodles with half of ricotta mixture, spread evenly
Cover with half of chicken mixture, spread evenly
Cover with 1 cup mozzarella cheese
Repeat all layers, noodles, ricotta mixture, chicken mixture, mozzarella cheese
Cover with layer of noodles
Cover noodles with last jar of Alfredo sauce
Cover top(s) with 1 cup of mozzarella on each 9" x 13" or 2 cups if using roasting pan
Bake until top is brown and bubbly, about 50-60 minutes
Slice, serve, and Mangia!

Lemon Basil Grilled Chicken

Use this however you like – it goes great on ciabatta rolls as a sandwich, over whatever pasta you have in your pantry, we've even had it over lemon basil pasta! Talk about layers of flavor! If using pasta and you want a simple sauce, just use $^1/_2$ cup of oil per pound of pasta. This can be straight $^1/_2$ cup of a quality olive oil, 1 stick of melted butter, or a mix of the two. Don't forget to add a little flavor to the sauce, even if it's just a few shakes of grated parmesan with a little ground black pepper. You don't want the sauce to outshine the chicken, just complement it.

6 boneless skinless chicken breasts (8 ounces each)
Zest from 2 lemons
Juice from 2 lemons
2 cloves garlic, run through garlic press
$^1/_2$ teaspoon salt
$^1/_4$ cup vegetable oil
1 package (0.75 ounce) fresh basil, chiffonade cut

Pound chicken to about $^1/_2$" thick
Pat chicken dry with paper towels
Place chicken in large resealable plastic bag
Add lemon zest, lemon juice, garlic, salt, and vegetable oil, and basil to bag
Massage bag to distribute marinade over all of the chicken
Marinate for at least 30 minutes, or even overnight in refrigerator
When ready to cook, preheat grill to med-high heat (about 400F)
Take chicken out of bag, discard marinade
Grill until chicken is cooked through, 150F, 6-7 minutes per side
Remove from grill and let rest for 3 minutes (for food safety)
Serve using method of choice and enjoy!

Oven Baked Chicken

Most of my recipes I have no idea who or where I got them from. This one is an exception. A Driver/Engineer I worked with throughout the years (from the great Mexican state of Nebraska – inside joke) used to make this on a pretty regular basis when it was his turn to cook. He claimed there was something special about the oven at the station, since it always came out perfect at the station but he said it never came out right at home. I have not seen the same effect, however – I've made this chicken many times at many stations as well as at home and had it come out excellent everywhere. As with other recipes made on a baking sheet, use non-stick foil or parchment paper, mainly to ease clean up. Placing the dark meat pieces around the outside exposes them to more heat than the middle, which helps them get to the higher temperature we want them to finish at.

2 Tablespoons salted butter, cut into pats
1 $^1/_2$ cups baking mix
1 $^1/_2$ Tablespoons paprika
1 Tablespoon season salt
$^1/_2$ teaspoon ground black pepper
2 cut up fryer chickens

Preheat oven to 425F
Melt butter on baking sheet in oven
Mix baking mix, paprika, season salt, and ground black pepper
Coat chicken in baking mix mixture
Pull baking sheet from oven when butter is melted
Place chicken skin side down on baking sheet, with dark meat around the outside
Bake 35 minutes, flip chicken
Bake 15 minutes longer, until breasts are 150F in middle
Remove from oven, rest for three minutes before serving
Enjoy!

Oven Fried Chicken

What could be more American than fried chicken? Okay, apple pie, but fried chicken is right up there. Here's a way to make a very convincing fried chicken without stinking up the station for two days. Even if mayonnaise isn't your thing, you're not using it for its flavor, you're using it for the eggs and oil that it's made from. As with other recipes made on a baking sheet, use non-stick foil, or parchment paper, or use non-stick cooking spray on the baking sheet to prevent sticking.

2 cut up fryer chickens
2 cups seasoned bread crumbs
2 teaspoons ground black pepper
2 teaspoons garlic powder
2 teaspoons season salt
2 teaspoons thyme
1 teaspoon paprika
2 cups mayonnaise

Preheat oven to 350F
In mixing bowl, mix bread crumbs, pepper, garlic powder, season salt, thyme, and paprika
Coat the chicken pieces with mayonnaise
Coat chicken pieces with bread crumb mixture
Place chicken pieces on a baking sheet with dark meat on outside
Bake until white meat is 150F and dark meat is 175F, about 45 minutes
Pull from oven, rest for three minutes
Serve and enjoy!

Thanksgiving Turkey

Thanksgiving is a fun time of year. For those of you with college age kids, you get to see them for usually the second time since the school year started, you get to see family members that you sometimes only see a few times a year, there's football on all day long, it's the one time of the year that an afternoon nap is tolerated, but there's also a ton of stress if you're the one cooking the turkey for dinner. It doesn't have to be that way, though. Dry brining helps keep the meat moist, while helping the skin get crispy. A spatchcocked bird simply means the backbone is removed, allowing the bird to be flatter while it cooks, helping to cook more evenly, quicker, and helps the skin get crispier. Cooking quicker means you don't have to get up at 4AM to get the bird going. Go ahead and take that nap, though – you've earned it, and let's face it, naps rock!

$^1/_2$ cup coarse kosher salt
2 Tablespoons baking powder
Fresh turkey, figure minimum one pound per person, spatchcocked
1 Tablespoon vegetable oil

The day before, mix the salt and the baking powder
Pat turkey dry with paper towels
Cover (not fully coat) turkey with salt mixture
Transfer turkey to a rack in a rimmed baking sheet
Refrigerate uncovered for 12-24 hours
Preheat oven to 450F, place rack in middle of oven
Rub entire skin with vegetable oil
Tuck wing tips behind back
Cook turkey on rack in baking sheet until breast reaches 150F, about 80 minutes
Pull from oven, remove from rack onto cutting board with juice groove
Let turkey rest for 20 minutes, carve, and enjoy both your meal and your nap!

Cooking at the Firehouse

Cooking at the firehouse in many ways is the same as cooking at home, however there are some big differences. Every department does things slightly different, here's how we did it in Rockford. Each shift at each station would either have one designated cook or just have everyone take turns. Each way has advantages and disadvantages. A designated cook usually is the best cook of the group, and is able to plan from day to day to save money here and there, which helps since everyone enjoying the meals shared in the cost. Having a designated cook also means you're stuck with their preferences. Most cooks, to an extent, will work around a particular crew member's likes and dislikes but that does get difficult with eight different personalities. Taking turns does often introduce a greater variety, since every firefighter has at least one recipe that they have down cold, but in the long run it usually ends up more expensive because you can't plan from day to day and use ingredients on multiple days.

There are two different funds that every firefighter had to pay into – the daily mess fund within their shift, and the station spice fund, which was collected either every payday or monthly. The daily mess fund was to repay the cook for the groceries they bought for that day, usually on their way in to work. Occasionally a crew would end up without a cook for the day so they would have to go to the store with the rig, but we tried to avoid that because you were still in service for calls and rarely were able to complete your shopping without interruption. The station spice fund went towards everything around the station that made it a firehouse. Coffee, the morning newspaper, TVs, butter, spices, peanut butter and jelly, internet, paper plates and napkins, condiments – they all came out of the spice fund. A savvy cook wouldn't spend shift mess money on seasoning mixes, instead making their own using the spices already on hand at the station. Just as important as a good cook was someone to run the spice fund well. After every meal, everyone would thank the cook, but the only time anyone ever said anything to the spice fund manager was when there was a complaint because we were out of something.

The department supplied a building to work out of, a kitchen with heavy duty equipment, and the basics for cooking with. If you wanted something special for cooking, either you bought it and kept it for only you to use, or held a vote for the spice fund to buy it and everyone could use it. Shifts that take turns cooking generally made do with just the basic equipment provided, while designated cooks tended to have specialty equipment that they kept for themselves. Good knives, an electric roaster, a waffle iron, a sous vide setup, a stand mixer, one cook even bought a heat lamp setup for his fried fish and onion rings.

Whenever you cooked, you had to be prepared for interruptions. When the alarm went off, you had to face the decision of whether to stop everything from cooking, or just turn some things down to low, and you had to make that decision within a few seconds. What you were cooking, where it was in the cooking process, what type of call it was and how long you expected to be gone all factored into your decision. All that, and you still wanted to be on the rig and out the door in less than 90 seconds. That sounds like a long time, but if you had to put all your gear on, that would eat up at least 60 of those seconds. On top of that, if you were the Driver/Engineer you had to be able to figure out where you were going and how to get there the quickest.

After the meal came washing the dishes. Every station did this differently. Some just had the new guys do it, my Lieutenant friend always cleaned the pots and pans and left everything else for the new guy, some stations played cards, one station traditionally rolled dice. I always preferred cards, giving the whole crew that much more time to bond together. I also liked cards because it usually took two wins to get out (with the last two playing stuck in the dishes) but the cook only needed one win. Since we weren't playing for money, there were some rather unique games: AK47, where aces, kings, 4s and 7s were wild, but all wild cards in your hand was a losing hand; Magnum, where 3s, 5s, and 7s were wild; low count, where you wanted the lowest total from adding up the values of the cards in your hand, and the ideal hand was all face cards because they counted as zero; tic tac toe, where everybody was dealt 5 cards, and nine community cards were arranged in a 3 x 3 matrix – everyone named their own wild card, and you had to make your best five card hand using two cards from your hand and any three cards in a row from the matrix, up and down, side to side, or diagonal.

Rubs, Seasonings, and Toppings

As mentioned previously, a savvy cook reduced his shifts mess budget by using ingredients paid for in the spice fund. Not only was there that advantage, but by making your own rubs, seasonings, and toppings, you were able to make them how you liked them, and sometimes healthier by not using as much salt, or not adding MSG. The recipes in this chapter were fine tuned over time to the way I (and my crews) liked them, but feel free to do your own experimenting to find the way you like them.

Buffalo Wing Rub

I used this when grilling chicken, before cooking and then coating with Buffalo sauce. I know people that have used this rub before smoking chicken, as well. I also have coated shrimp with this seasoning, you can use it anytime you want to add a little smoky, sweet heat to something.

$^1/_2$ cup dark brown sugar
2 Tablespoons garlic powder
2 Tablespoons salt (or to taste)
1 Tablespoon ground black pepper
1 Tablespoon chili powder (recipe on page 160)
1 Tablespoon cumin
1 Tablespoon dry mustard powder
1 Tablespoon paprika
1 teaspoon cayenne pepper

Mix all ingredients, coat chicken before cooking on the grill

Cajun Seasoning

There are many premade cajun seasonings out there, but I always thought they were either too salty, or too spicy, so I settled on this mix that was just right in my opinion. Your mileage may vary, maybe I'm just a wimp and you want more heat, go for it! If you're making this to have on hand, go ahead and use pre ground black pepper, but if making it for immediate use, definitely use fresh ground pepper if you can.

$^1/_4$ cup garlic powder
$^1/_4$ cup oregano flakes
$^1/_4$ cup paprika
2 Tablespoons onion powder
2 Tablespoons salt
Heaping Tablespoon cayenne pepper
Heaping Tablespoon ground black pepper

Mix all ingredients, use as much or as little as you like on whatever you like!

Candied Jalapenos

Another Vermont connection here. In the town of Shelburne, VT., a wood fired brick oven pizza place known as Folino's shares a building with an awesome brewery, Fiddlehead. Folino's is a BYOB pizza place, so in order to succeed, the pizza has to be on point – spoiler alert, it is. Last time we were there, with the normal pizza condiments such as crushed red peppers, oregano, and parmesan, they had candied jalapenos. Being the curious type, I tried a small amount on a slice of pizza, and after tasting it, I immediately searched the internet for a recipe, which I found on brooklynfarmgirl.com. Not only does this go excellent on pizza, but pretty much anything else benefits from the slightly sweet, slightly fruity, not too spicy addition of some candied jalapenos. If even a little heat is too much for you, in addition to removing the seeds, remove the ribs (where most of the heat is) and scrape the inside of the fruit (where the rest of the heat is).

12 jalapeno peppers, seeded, sliced or diced
1 cup white sugar
$1/2$ cup water

Place jalapenos in a small pan, add sugar and water
Heat over med-high heat until boiling
Reduce to simmer
Stirring occasionally, let simmer until liquid reduces to syrup (30-60 minutes)
Let cool and store in jar in refrigerator
Mix into hamburgers, serve with cheese on a cracker, top your pizza, however you want to enjoy it!

Chili Powder

I don't know what I was thinking, but I used to think chili powder was just a spice, until I found out it was a mixture of other spices. Once I found that out, I started experimenting until I came up with the flavor I was looking for adding to my meals. If you have a spice grinder, go ahead and give it a whirl so all the components are the same size and mixed more thoroughly.

$1/4$ cup paprika
Heaping Tablespoon oregano flakes
1 Tablespoon cumin
1 Tablespoon garlic powder
1 $1/2$ teaspoons onion powder
1 teaspoon cayenne pepper

Mix all ingredients thoroughly, keep on hand for whenever you need it!

Fajita Seasoning

This can be used on any protein you want in your fajitas, just sprinkle it on and cook however you like – grilled, sauteed, on a baking sheet, however!

3 Tablespoons corn starch
2 Tablespoons chili powder (recipe on page 160)
1 Tablespoon paprika
1 Tablespoon salt
1 Tablespoon white sugar
1 $1/2$ teaspoon ground cumin
1 $1/2$ teaspoon garlic powder
1 $1/2$ teaspoon onion powder
$3/4$ teaspoon cayenne pepper

Mix all ingredients, sprinkle liberally on both protein and veggies for fajitas

Montreal Steak Seasoning

Montreal steak seasoning was actually created in Montreal, allegedly by a broilerman at a deli that used the Eastern European influenced pickling spices they coated their meat with before smoking on his steaks and it caught on with the customers. Once word got out all the spice companies made their own versions. I use this on steaks, burgers, chicken, pork, veggies, pretty much anything! I like doing bigger pieces of the spices and crushing while mixing until I get the size particles I like.

2 Tablespoons ground black pepper
1 Tablespoon dill
1 Tablespoon dried garlic flakes
1 Tablespoon dried onion flakes
1 Tablespoon paprika
1 Tablespoon crushed red pepper flakes
1 Tablespoon coarse salt
2 teaspoons coriander
2 teaspoons dry mustard seeds

Rib Rub

This goes great not only on pork ribs, but any pork, or beef, or chicken for that matter. You can also dry brine the ribs like a turkey – if you do, leave the salt out of the rub.

$^1/_3$ cup brown sugar
1 Tablespoon paprika
1 Tablespoon ground black pepper
1 Tablespoon salt
2 teaspoons garlic powder

Mix all ingredients, coat meat liberally

Sazon

This is the spice mix I like to use when making tacos or carne asada. You can buy the premade stuff, but some people don't like the MSG in it so I use this. It was also advantageous money wise to make my own since most of the ingredients came out of the spice fund. 2 ¹/₂ Tablespoons per pound of meat is a good place to start, if you want more flavor, then by all means go heavier, if it's a bit too much for you then use less.

3 Tablespoons annatto
3 Tablespoons cumin
3 Tablespoons coriander
3 Tablespoons garlic powder
3 Tablespoons salt
2 Tablespoons oregano
1 Tablespoon onion powder
1 Tablespoon ground black pepper

Mix all ingredients, grind, store in airtight container

Taco Seasoning

Some people have stomach issues after eating foods containing annatto (my wife) so I also have this recipe for making tacos. I usually brown the meat, drain the grease, then return the meat to the skillet and stir in the taco seasoning mixed with ½ cup water. One Tablespoon per $^1/_2$ pound is a good starting point, but experiment and find the level you and your family like.

$^1/_3$ cup chili powder (recipe on page 160)
3 Tablespoons cumin
2 Tablespoons ground black pepper
2 Tablespoons salt
1 Tablespoon paprika
1 $^1/_2$ teaspoons garlic powder
1 $^1/_2$ teaspoons onion powder
1 $^1/_2$ teaspoons oregano
1 $^1/_2$ teaspoons crushed red pepper flakes

Mix all ingredients, crush to particle size you like

Tartar Sauce

You can buy tartar sauce at the store, but with how much fish costs and the budget I had, I preferred making my own. It was an added bonus that I was able to make it just the way I wanted. Funny thing about tartar sauce, I had never even tried it until I was on the fire department (I grew up only squeezing lemon juice onto my fish), and eventually I became a snob about my tartar sauce!

1 cup mayonnaise
2 teaspoons sweet pickle relish
1 teaspoon lemon juice
1 teaspoon mustard of choice

Mix all ingredients together, serve with fish

Fire Department Ranks

The Fire Department is a paramilitary organization, dependent on the chain of command, which obviously necessitates a chain of command. Not all departments have all of the ranks, some call the same ranks by different names, while some also use the conventional insignia for other ranks. Generally, the larger a department is, the more ranks it will have.

All firefighters start off as probationary firefighters, sometimes referred to as probies or FNGs. Most often, probies will have attended a fire academy and received the basics of how to fight fires, but no two fires are the same. Their career long learning starts here, under the tutelage of their crew.

After a period of time, probationary firefighters lose the probationary part of their title and become firefighters. Most departments require their firefighters to be EMTs, if not paramedics leading to the titles firefighter/EMT or firefighter/paramedic. Firefighters comprise the highest number of people in any rank on the department, with anywhere from two to seven or more assigned to each company on each shift. For most firefighters, this is the title they will carry for more time than any other title during their career.

The position of Driver/Engineer is a tricky one. Some departments fill the Driver/Engineer spot by seniority, some by testing, and still others have no official Driver/Engineer rank but pay acting Driver/Engineer pay to the senior firefighter on each company each day. Driver/Engineers are responsible for the apparatus assigned to the company, as well as any equipment, and usually are the insulation between the crew and their officer. By insulation, I mean that if there are any issues, the firefighters go to the Driver, and only if he/she can't solve the issue, then it goes to the officer. In most departments, Driver/Engineer is the highest rank that is a "blue shirt," somewhat like a Sergeant is the highest ranking enlisted rank in the military.

The officers' ranks starts off with Lieutenants, which are signified by single silver bugles on their collar. Lieutenants are usually the first rank that wears a white shirt instead of the Firefighter and Driver/Engineer blue shirt. Although different in some departments, Lieutenants are generally in charge of one shift of one company at one station. Lieutenants are responsible for determining the course of action at an emergency scene, completing the paperwork necessary after the emergency is over, planning the various activities the company must do throughout the year, such as hose testing, hydrant testing, inspections, training, etc...

Captains are the next up on the totem pole. Captains wear two upright silver bugles on their collar, although some departments use two crossed silver bugles. Captains not only have the same responsibilities as a Lieutenant for the crew on their shift day, but Captains are also responsible for the station as a whole, including things such as ordering supplies needed, planning the station activities that will be performed and how often they are performed, and anything else the station needs in the opinion of the Captain.

The next step up introduces us to the gold bugle and white helmet club. A Battalion Chief sports two crossed gold bugles on their collar, and is responsible for the daily activities of a group of stations and the companies located in those stations. Battalions are organized by geographic location, and the Battalion Chief responds to major emergencies in their battalion, such as structure fires, mass medical events, hazardous materials emergencies, pretty much any time there are more than two apparatus responding. On the emergency scenes, the Battalion Chief takes over command of the incident from the first arriving officer. Some departments refer to battalions as districts, making the Battalion Chief a District Chief.

District Chiefs wear three crossed gold bugles on their collar, and are responsible for a group of battalions the same way a Battalion Chief is responsible for a group of companies. District Chiefs are the highest rank that still works the firefighter shift schedule, and generally are responsible for the daily manning within their district. If one company has too few people, then the District Chief must figure out if another company has too many people so they can temporarily reassign someone to the shorthanded company or if they have to pay overtime to someone to fill out the company.

Division Chiefs wear four crossed gold bugles, and are the first of two levels that work a 40 hour week. Division Chiefs are responsible for separate functions of the Fire Department, such as Administration, Inspection, Maintenance, Operations (including EMS Operations, Fire Operations, Special Operations), and Training. These chiefs are responsible for establishing and enforcing the rules applying to their division.

Department Chiefs wear five crossed gold bugles (since this is the highest number of bugles, sometimes the Department Chief is referred to as "Chief All Bugles") and is responsible for all of the activities of the entire department. While the Division Chiefs are each responsible for their division, it is the Department Chief that decides the overall tone of the department and has final say on any rules the Division Chiefs establish.

Some larger departments have a rank above Department Chief called Commissioner. Although generally the Commissioner is a civilian position appointed by the mayor, it is not unusual to have a very senior member of the department in this post. The Commissioner is responsible for going between the city and the department, obtaining the funding for the things the Department Chief would like to institute.

Desserts

Desserts weren't a part of daily life around the firehouse. Other than finding ice cream in the freezer from someone's overtime treats, dessert usually was from someone bringing it in to celebrate their birthday. Some stations wrapped dessert up with the twice daily card games, keeping track of who the two losers were, and the biggest loser at the end of the month had to bring in a dessert. There were also times where we just plain had a rough day, and someone decided they would make dessert to help pick everybody's mood up. Entire books have been written dedicated to dessert recipes, here's my favorites.

Bread Pudding

I used to hide the leftover bread in the freezer and when I had enough I would make bread pudding, until someone else found my stash and used it for croutons. Then I started buying bread specifically for bread pudding, and one morning wondered how it would taste with Hawaiian bread. Since it made the cookbook, obviously it went over well!

2 packages (18 ounces each) Hawaiian style dinner rolls
$^3/_4$ cup raisins
$^1/_2$ cup salted butter, melted
2 teaspoons ground cinnamon
12 eggs
1 $^1/_2$ cups white sugar
1 Tablespoon and 1 teaspoon vanilla extract
1 teaspoon salt
6 cups hot milk (160F)
$^1/_4$ teaspoon nutmeg

Preheat oven to 200F
Shred dinner rolls into large chunks, spread in one layer on baking sheet
Put shredded rolls in oven for 60 minutes to dry rolls out
Remove shredded rolls from oven, preheat oven to 375
Grease the bottom of a roasting pan
In a mixing bowl, combine shredded rolls, raisins, butter, and cinnamon
Pour roll mixture into greased roasting pan
Beat together eggs, sugar, vanilla, and salt
Pour over shredded rolls
Sprinkle with nutmeg, cook until top is golden brown and middle is somewhat firm, about 25 – 30 minutes
Serve and enjoy the yummy goodness!

Chocolate Éclair Cake

This simple recipe has been around forever, and for good reason! Perfect for the depths of Summer, since there's no need to turn the oven on and heat up the kitchen.

3 cups milk
1 container (8 ounce) frozen whipped topping, thawed
2 packages (3.5 ounces each) instant vanilla pudding mix
1 box (16 ounce) graham cracker squares
1 package (16 ounce) prepared chocolate frosting

Stir milk, whipped topping, and pudding mix together in mixing bowl
Lay a single layer of graham crackers in the bottom of a 9" x 13" pan
Spread half of the milk mix over crackers
Lay another layer of graham crackers on top of milk mix
Spread remaining half of milk mix over graham crackers
Top with final layer of graham crackers
Spread the frosting over the whole cake
Cover, refrigerate at least 4 hours, serve and dig in!

Mock Apple Pie

A pie made from crackers? Why would anyone want to even try that, much less who came up with the idea in the first place? It is believed that the British Navy first started making mock fruit pies a couple of centuries ago to take plain crackers, which last a long time, and make them into not only something different from what they were, but make them into a treat. Mock apple pie would make a resurgence whenever fresh apples were either in short supply or tremendously expensive, such as during wartime or the Great Depression. It's hard to believe, but it really does taste and feel like an apple pie. There's science behind why, but let's forget about science and get cooking!

2 cups water
1 cup white sugar
2 teaspoons cream of tartar
36 buttery round crackers
1 Tablespoon lemon juice
1 teaspoon cinnamon, divided
1 prepared 9" pie shell
1 cup crushed buttery round crackers
$^1/_2$ cup brown sugar
$^1/_3$ cup salted butter, melted

Preheat oven to 425F
In saucepan over med-high heat, combine water, sugar, and cream of tartar
Bring mixture to a boil
Drop in whole crackers and boil for 5 minutes
Pour mixture into pie shell, Sprinkle with lemon juice and ½ teaspoon cinnamon
Mix together crushed crackers, brown sugar, butter, and remaining cinnamon
Sprinkle cracker mix over pie filling
Bake for 15 minutes, reduce oven to 375 and bake for 15 – 20 more minutes
Serve warm, top with whipped cream, and watch everyone's face when you tell them there's no apples in it!

Pineapple Upside Down Cake

Way back when, a new guy (Grandpa Art) started on the fire department on a Sunday. He wanted to make a special dessert for his crew, because it was his first day, and because they had to work on a Sunday. The only dessert he knew how to make was pineapple upside down cake. Two weeks later, when they worked on a Sunday again, his crew made it abundantly clear they wanted pineapple upside down cake again. So it went every Sunday, and soon it spread to the other stations in the city. For decades, every station in town made pineapple upside down cake every Sunday, and as is often the case with traditions, very few people know how the tradition started.

$^1/_2$ cup butter
1 $^1/_2$ cups brown sugar
1 can (20 ounce) sliced pineapple
10 Maraschino cherries
1 box (18.25 ounce) white cake mix

Melt the butter in an iron skillet over med-high heat
Pull off the heat, sprinkle brown sugar evenly to cover the butter
Arrange the pineapple rings around the bottom of the pan in a single layer
Place a cherry in the middle of each pineapple ring
Substituting pineapple juice for an equivalent amount of liquid, prepare the cake mix according to the directions on the box
Pour the batter over the pineapple layer
Bake as directed in the cake mix directions
After pulling from oven, let cool for 10 minutes
Remove from pan to a plate (If you let cake cool too much it will stick to pan)
Serve, and let working on a Sunday be just a little better with dessert!

Pumpkin Bars

I have a little secret to share with you – I cannot stand pumpkin pie. Period. I don't know why, but I have never been able to stomach it. One year, just before Thanksgiving one of the local TV stations had a lighthearted competition between the police and fire departments, involving frozen turkey bowling, and various other events including a pumpkin pie eating contest. The contest was done like a relay, with each member of each team eating a slice of pumpkin pie before the next member could start. I told my teammates that I needed to be last in line, and needed to be right next to a garbage can. When I tried to eat my slice, luckily the camera wasn't on me, but you could still hear the slice not stay in my stomach, but go into the garbage can. Having said all that, these bars are FANTASTIC! More like an orange colored brownie, I have no problem eating more of these than I should.

1 can (15 ounce) pumpkin
1 cup vegetable oil
4 eggs, beaten
2 cups all purpose flour
2 teaspoons baking powder
1 $1/2$ teaspoons cinnamon
1 teaspoon baking soda
$1/2$ teaspoon salt
2 $1/2$ cups powdered sugar
$3/4$ cup salted butter, softened
3 ounces cream cheese, softened
1 teaspoon vanilla extract

Preheat oven to 350F
Beat together pumpkin, oil, and eggs
Sift together flour, baking powder, cinnamon, and baking soda
Mix above together, pour onto 11" x 15" baking sheet, bake for 30 minutes
Cool on counter after pulling from oven
For icing, beat powdered sugar, butter, cream cheese, and vanilla
Spread icing over baked pumpkin mix when it cools
Slice and enjoy a nice Autumn day! (No matter what season it is)

Strawberry Pretzel Salad

Not too sweet, not too salty, this classic really impresses when you make it in a glass casserole dish! Usually not a problem, but you want to eat it as soon as you can after it finishes in the refrigerator, otherwise the pretzels get soggy.

2 cups crushed hard snack pretzels
$^3/_4$ cup salted butter, melted
1 cup and 3 Tablespoons white sugar, divided
1 package (8 ounce) cream cheese, softened
1 container (8 ounce) frozen whipped topping, thawed
2 packages (3 ounces each) strawberry flavored gelatin
2 cups boiling water
2 packages (10 ounces each) frozen strawberries

Preheat oven to 400F
Mix crushed pretzels, melted butter, and 3 Tablespoons sugar well
Press pretzel mixture into bottom of a 9" x 13" baking dish
Bake 8 to 10 minutes, set aside to cool
In large mixing bowl, mix cream cheese and sugar
Fold in whipped topping
Spread cream cheese/topping mixture on cooled crust
Dissolve gelatin in boiling water
Stir in frozen strawberries and allow to set briefly
When mixture thickens slightly, pour and spread over cream cheese layer
Refrigerate until set
Slice, serve, and enjoy!

178